Why I'm Not Afraid to Die

What a Crow and a Near Death Experience Taught Me

A Mystical Journey to Healing & Nourishment for the Soul

Dr. Dawn Cormier, HBSc.,
www.naturopathichealthandwellnesscentre.com
dcormier2222@gmail.com

Dedication

To the Unified Field of Pure Love and Light all around us and within us, for the whispers of guidance, unconditional love, and support.

To my mother, for midwifing me back into my body, nurturing and supporting me in the way only a mother can.

To my partner in marriage, for all your unwavering care, love, guidance, and support in my healing journey back to wholeness.

To Daniel Blasutti, my first patient with cancer who died and crossed the rainbow bridge. He was my teacher in death and life. Thank you for seeing me and gifting me my spiritual name **"Crow Woman"** – one who helps souls pass over and transition to the spiritual worlds.

Contents

Dedication 3
Introduction 7
Prologue 11
Chapter One - Home Sweet Home 15
    The Crash: A Glimpse Across The Veil 18
    The Aftermath: Picking Up the Pieces 22
Chapter Two - The Road Home to Wholeness and Healing 27
    Coming Full Circle: Following the Mystical Path 30
Chapter Three - A Little Bit About Spirit Animals, Guides & Totems 37
    Crow: My Spirit Guide and Totem 38
    My Lesson from Spirit 41
    Listening to Spirit and Our Guides 44
    Your Inner Guidance System 45
Chapter Four - Why I'm Not Afraid To Die 51
    My NDE Showed Me That Our End is Not "The End" 52
    This is what I've come to know about death 56
    What Else Prompted Me to Write This Book? 58
    What about Worry and Fear? 62
Chapter Five - Treasure in Your Trauma 65
    Human Trauma & The Meaning of Suffering 66
    A Hero's Example 71
    Where Do We Go from Here? 72

Chapter Six - The Path Forward 75
    How Do I Know What Is My Path? 77
    Tuning into Your Soul's Inner Guidance 78
    The Three Minds and The Three Energy Centres 79
    Why Didn't I Remember All of This Coming Into This Lifetime? 83
    Remembrances to Nourish Your Soul 85

Appendix 89
    3:3:6 Breath 90
    Morning Greeting to Great Spirit 90
    Morning Declaration 91
    Prayer for Spiritual Connection & Support 92
    Declaration of your I AM Presence 93
    Gratitude for Divine Presence 93
    Calling in the Angels 93
    Awakened Consciousness Prayer 94
    Transforming Worry into Peace and Acceptance 95
        Method one: Awareness 95
        Method two: Heart Command 95
    Sip of the Divine 96
    Blessing Everything Meditation 97
    Healing "I am Word" Declaration 99
    Heart Coherence Practice 100

Introduction

One day, while sitting in sacred meditation, the Angels told me, "It is time to share your story. People need this message now."

This auditory message was so strong and clear that I couldn't say no, and it resulted in what you are about to read. This is the story of my near-death experience (NDE) and my mystical journey to healing. I share it openly from the depths of my heart. It is my hope that it opens the doors of remembrance and nourishes every soul who reads this book. May it remind you to listen to – and honour – your soul and your truth. May it serve as a guide on your journey as you recall your true nature: the Spirit of Pure Love and Light that you are.

My glimpse of Heaven will clarify why I am not afraid to die, and perhaps inspire you also to live and die without fear.

Dear friends,

    This story of my personal near-death experience comes to these pages pure and untainted by outside influences. I do not consider myself an expert on NDEs, nor did I study or research NDEs prior to writing this book. The truth is, I have only read one account of an NDE quite by chance years ago – Anita Moorjani's book, Dying to Be Me. Her book was gifted to me by a dear friend. I thoroughly enjoyed her story and found it relatable and inspiring. Reading about her NDE was a blessing, and I thank Anita from the bottom of my heart for having the courage and vulnerability to share her story. I know there are many NDE stories out there you could choose to read. I am honoured you chose to read this one and I sincerely hope the messages, insights, and experiences in this book will serve you well.

To sum up what you're about to embark upon, this book is the story of how it took a Near Death Experience, my spirit guide (a crow), and several soul-inspired and mystical events to set me on my soul's path and bring about my physical healing. These life experiences served and enabled me to keep searching for the meaning in my trauma and for ways to heal my body. This journey inevitably led me through a spiritual awakening that equipped me to assist others on their healing journeys, and to find deeper meaning in my role as a Doctor of Naturopathic Medicine and a Modern Mystic. In fact, the pain and injuries I sustained from the car crash definitely kept me humble and on course with my soul's compass in so many ways.

If this book does not resonate with you, it is completely okay. I trust in the consciousness of all and I am a firm believer that each of us walks our own unique path in our own Divine timing. I have had to honour my own Divine timing every step along my journey as well. For instance, I have read some of the most incredible compilations from inspired authors, taken hundreds of courses in self-development, all the while hoping and believing they would catapult me to the next level of my spiritual development. However, that was not always the case, and not always the right timing. Sometimes the approach, the words, and the resonance of the teaching didn't land in incredible ways or spark remembrances until I was truly ready. And sometimes it was not so much the timing, but the alignment of the information that was critical in my evolutionary process. So please, my friends, run these words and this story through your own discernment. Feel them with your whole heart - the sacred seat of your Divine Soul. Follow your own compass. If this book helps you in any way to open up your experience with Spirit and not fear death or illness, then I've accomplished what I set out to do.

I have learned many lessons in my life that may help you in yours. These are a few of them: trust your inner guidance; hold everything with an open heart; nothing bad happens that doesn't offer something good; other people's opinions of you don't define you, but your stories do; and, suffering is in the human mind and has nothing to do with circumstances and events in your life. Most of all, be loving, merciful and compassionate with yourself. This journey is yours. People may judge you, but do not fear this or become frustrated with it in any way. Your life is your soul's gift of evolution to you. Embrace it, with all the ups and downs, because this is what you are here to experience.

For the most part, many of us perceive our reality from the vantage point of a familiar belief structure – often one that has been handed down for generations. Our beliefs are deeply tied to our culture, theological teachings, and personal experiences. They become embedded and adopted as values that influence our choices, behaviours, and everything really. For example, I was raised in a Roman Catholic family. The teachings around death and eternity are ones that many of you can probably relate to: *"If you are good, you go to heaven. If you are bad, you spend all of eternity in hell."* Teachings like these can indeed help us create a moral code that guides our actions and decisions in life. On the other hand, they can also lead to a life motivated by fear, control, and judgments – a recipe for stress, anxiety, worry and illness.

I promise you, if you come on this ride with me open-heartedly, your awareness will expand and you will be transformed by the Light within you. Heaven awaits you now and in the next world.

- What if you had an experience in life that shattered all preconceived notions of **Death** and the **After Life**?
- What if you had an NDE that completely took you out of your comfort zone and opened you up to a whole new reality, where you now saw the world as a **safe** and **Holy Place**?
- What if you could shift your view of the dying process and feel comfort knowing that the after-life is one of peace and bliss?
- What if you come to know yourself as a Divine Soul in a Sacred human body?

- What if you become aware of the helpful and compassionate Spirits beyond the veil who are here with you always, loving, guiding, and supporting you?
- What if you begin seeing the events in life as gifts instead of disasters?
- What if you tell yourself a different story around your trauma?
- Would you agree that this could change your core beliefs dramatically, possibly leading you to live your life from a place of **Soulful Divine Knowing** and **Love**?
- What if we could, in fact, create Heaven on Earth?
- What if you could share this wisdom with your loved ones?

As humans, we often require a little shaking up in our lives for us to change, and for us to see and adopt new perspectives. I promise, if you had a NDE it would revolutionize the way you understand your existence and our collective consciousness. It would definitely impact how you live your life. But not everyone has had, or will have, the benefit of this gift. You don't need an NDE to jolt you into this new reality. I would like to share with you my experience to help you understand the miracle you truly are, and perhaps open you to new or alternative beliefs. When we change how we view the world, this fundamentally changes our reality. And when we change ourselves, we change the world and our collective consciousness; we all evolve together.

I hope that my story, with the struggles and opportunities life has served up for me, will be a catalyst, a remembrance, a support, and perhaps a light for you on your journey back to wholeness. My further hope is that my story may inspire you on your awakening journey and guide you home to the truth of who and what you really are.

Come with me as we break the habits and constructs that have kept us captive and unaware of our Light. Are you ready to open your consciousness?

Prologue

My Spiritual journey has affirmed for me that I come from a long lineage of medicine women, midwives, mystics, and healers. This lifetime, once again, was dedicated to healing and the mystical path.

At a very early age, I saw and experienced the world differently from most of my family and friends. This didn't make me better than anyone else at all. In fact, I often felt isolated, different, marginalized, ridiculed, and downright confused by most of our cultural norms and expectations. Despite the harshness of the human condition, I somehow had a different awareness. It shaped my beliefs and perceptions of people and the world around me. I didn't try to be different or difficult. I just had a deep knowing – a remembrance of something other than what I'd been taught – and I couldn't shake it.

As a child, I often escaped to nature to be with the trees, plants, water, and animals. That's where I felt the safest. Sometimes I would lie down and fall asleep in the forest, feeling at home and fully supported by Mother Nature. I could see and talk with the elementals (fairies, gnomes, plant spirits, and animals). So excited from my interactions, I would come home and tell my mother all about my friends and what they had said to me. Her response: "Stop making up such stories and go wash your hands for dinner." No one believed me, but I knew they existed.

At night, friendly angels and spirits visited me in my bedroom. They would sit on my bed or on my windowsill, and we'd have a great time hanging out. I soon learned not to speak out loud of my magical friends to avoid scorn and judgment. Even though as an adult I now know that I (and so many others) could see and experience spirits in other dimensions or across the veil. Sadly, the world wasn't ready for full disclosure of our nature elementals and the many spiritual worlds around us. It wasn't "normal" or culturally acceptable to chatter on about such things. Yet, I believe today these kinds of childhood experiences are embraced far more easily than 50 years ago. The hippie, tree hugging era had just started up when I was a child in the 1960s. Today, we are much more open to concepts of energy, angels, and spirits. The time is ripe for awakening and transformation.

I grew up in a world steeped with generations of social constructs that didn't make any sense to me (war, famine, suppression, racism, inequality, separation, segregation, abuse, extremes of wealth and poverty, inadequate educational systems, a broken medical system, the spraying of toxic pesticides and chemicals, all the fear of illness and death, etc.). It often left me feeling sad and bewildered. No disrespect intended, but growing up in a Catholic home was very challenging and sometimes disheartening for me. On a daily basis, I questioned all the theological teachings and values of the times, and was met with punitive, sometimes shaming reactions from teachers and leaders in the church.

The programs in my head were incongruent with my heart. I constantly heard, "Just do as you're told." Or, in answer to my questions, "Just because. That's the way it is." When the adults in my life shut down my curiosity and questioning of the status quo, my heart would sink every time. Deep down, it knew a different reality – one not quite so tangible or obvious to the average human, but real nonetheless. I guess you could say I lived one foot in the higher dimensions and spiritual worlds and one foot in our 3-dimensional world. I was mostly (but not always) aware of our multi-dimensional reality and truth. It was common for me to astral travel out of my body and see spirits around me. I could feel a person's emotions before they spoke the words. This was difficult for a sensitive, empathic mystical little human like me. Maybe many of you reading this can relate.

In our present times, humanity is under extreme pressure (economically, environmentally, politically, spiritually) and this is providing the perfect opportunity for punctuated evolution as a species on this Earth. However, **it all comes down to how you choose to look at it**. You can choose to believe that the world is in great peril, or you can choose to see that it's a time of evolutionary change, expansion, ascension and spiritual awakening. Some call it awakening to a 5th Dimensional reality. Some call it the coming of the Aquarian Age, some the Golden Age, and some claim that it's the Rapture. Others say it's the time of the Divine Feminine, and She now holds the reins for our future as a species on this planet. Still others say that it's our time of ushering in Heaven on Earth. Whichever way you look at it, if we are living on this beautiful planet, we are here for the ride.

This is the end of a 12,000 year cycle, and this is our time as sensitives. We are evolving into The Age of Light Consciousness. During this evolutionary shift into an ascended consciousness, we will come to know the Truth of who we really are. Whether it is slow or fast in coming, we are all being asked to take responsibility for our own healing from lifetimes and past generations. By healing our own trauma, we assist each other, and together we can ascend and evolve as a species. Healing these distortions and densities will allow us to hold a larger light quotient. It will awaken us to our spiritual truths and help us make the shift from "Homo sapiens" to "Homo luminous." When one is lifted up, we are all lifted up. This is the time for humans to embody our Truth – that we are all Spirits of Pure Love and Light, formless and infinite in nature. We are truly a Divine spark of Creation, or God.

Chapter One

Home Sweet Home

I was born in North Bay, Ontario, Canada – fondly called the "Gateway to the North." Although my parents moved our family south to the Mississauga area when I was 6 years old, I spent every holiday and most of my summers in North Bay with Nana and Nono. This felt like my true home. Growing up with our Italian family, my early years were shaped by endless fun, love, and adventure. I was very lucky.

My Nono, a full-on entertainer, was always putting on skits, and doing voice overs to the old movie reels of Ali Baba, and Disney's Daffy Duck. He was essentially a big kid, and I loved everything about him, including the mix of his vanilla-scented pipe tobacco and the bug spray smell in his workshop. Nono was a professional hockey player in his younger years. He retired to the North, where he raised a big family. An avid outdoorsman, he taught me to appreciate the northern bush country and nature. We had many adventures at remote bush camps and wonderful walks in the northern trails. Just being in nature felt like being closer to God.

My Nana was the glue of the family, and truly an embodiment of Mother Mary herself. A kind, gentle, loving grandmother, her hugs were healing in their own right. She still, to this day, visits me in dream time and we share hugs with each other. She taught me about God and exemplified unconditional love, acceptance, honour, and respect. When I had questions about life, such as, "Why would God let this (fill in the blank) happen to people, Nana?" she would patiently sit me down and give me her understanding and explanation, steeped in Roman Catholicism and backed by a heart full of compassion. She never expected or demanded that we say prayers with her, but every evening, we had an open invitation to say the rosary with her. I enjoyed sharing in her quiet, reverent form of faith. Looking back, I realize later in life that counting all those beads and focusing on God was a form of meditation. During these precious times, she helped me see and feel the spiritual assistance available to us, and all around us. Meditative prayer taught me that we are but a thin veil away from our celestial helpers and God doesn't live in a church; God is within all of us.

If Nana was not cooking or cleaning, she could undoubtedly be found at church, where she faithfully lead the choir. Her default question throughout her life was, "What would love do?" I watched her love and support everyone in her world. She gave meaning to unconditional love in action. Professionally, she was a nurse who left the profession to raise a family of six children, and many grandchildren and great grandchildren. Nana was my line in the sand. If I couldn't look her in the eye regarding something I had done, then I knew it wasn't right. Together, Nana and Nono represented the most loving couple I've ever met in my life, to this day. I will hang onto the feeling and experience of being with them, always and forever.

My mother, Dianne, was in her second marriage to my stepfather Ralph when they retired to Trout Lake in North Bay. Their cabin, a peaceful place on God's beautiful planet, became the hub of many visiting family and friends. If anyone showed up unexpectedly, it was not unusual to find a "Gone Fishing" sign on the door. We were always welcome. Grandpa Ralph was a favourite with the grandchildren. His gentle heart (and love for ice cream) won them over in a heartbeat. Mom was the organizer of the family and took care of everyone. If you were ever sick or needed care in any way, you wanted her to be in charge. She would have made a wonderful nurse, like her mom. Instinctively, she had all the skills to comfort you and care for you, and you always felt safe.

Many would say that Mom was a complex person. She had her fair share of emotional wounds she carried in her lifetime. I am keenly aware that our soul contract together was strong and fierce. When I was young, she began suffering from stomach ulcers. To her credit, and before it was a popular thing to do, she started going to meditation classes to manage her stress, and she dragged me along. I would find myself in a home with a bunch of older ladies doing meditations one night a week. Afterwards we listened to Neil Diamond records and had tea. Honestly, I loved it. I had many wondrous and ethereal experiences there, even some out-of-body ones, which sparked my curiosity to dive deeper into the mystical unseen worlds.

My mother introduced me to lots of metaphysical ideas and concepts, and invited me to engage, attend classes, read books, and visit psychics. Her book case was full of Tarot books, and authors like Bernie Siegel, Wayne Dyer, Leo Buscaglia, Eckhart Tolle, Rumi, Edgar Casey, Emily Rosa, and the Dalai Lama. She took me to my first Therapeutic Touch course in the 1980s, taught by an aboriginal nurse in Toronto. I can't thank her enough for this amazing introduction to energy healing. It was one of her biggest gifts to me. I started to understand the innate healing power of life force energy that we all have, and how to start using it. I use it in my work today, and am now a Reiki Master, Qigong Practitioner, and modern-day Mystical Healer.

My mother (along with my Higher Self) also inspired me to enroll in Naturopathic Medicine College and become an energy healer, at a time when everyone else around me was skeptical. Later in her life, Mom developed Meniere's disease and was cured through the care of a Naturopathic Doctor. Once again, her life experience was showing me the way.

I am sharing this backdrop with you as a context for how I grew up – in a wonderful and loving home. While not perfectly idyllic, it set the stage for my journey. It was within this context that I willingly made the decision to betray myself and not listen to my higher guidance. On that fateful winter night, I chose to get in the car and drive South to return for work the next day. That drive ended in a car crash, and my life-changing Near-Death Experience (NDE).

The Crash: A Glimpse Across The Veil

My oldest daughter Samantha and I have been best travel buddies since she was just a few weeks old. When she was younger, we loved to spontaneously pack up and hop in our Suzuki Sidekick to go visit the family up North. I knew that road like the back of my hand. With the number of trips we made, I'm sure my car could have driven itself there and back. Sam and I would always start our adventures by playing our Willie Nelson CD and his song, "On the Road Again." She loved it and so did I. It meant freedom and fun.

On that fateful day, five-year-old Samantha and I were wrapping up a wonderful visit at the lake with Mom and Grandpa Ralph. It was time to pack up and head home. I had that familiar Sunday angst about going back to work on Monday. The feeling overshadowed the beauty of what Sunday still had to offer. My mind kept pulling me out of the present moment and into the future. As I was packing up the car, I felt more and more sadness about having to leave family and this piece of heaven. As Sunday drew to a close, the intense desire to stay turned into an eerie longing in my soul.

Usually, I would leave North Bay in the daylight, and always before dinner and sunset, especially in the winter. With the snow and ice, the roads up North could get very dicey within minutes. This time, I prolonged my departure beyond my usual time frame. In fact, even though I knew it was late in the day, I decided to stop by Nana's house for dinner. The gang was all there, and it was another chance to fill my cup with a delicious home cooked Italian meal and the love of family.

We said goodbye to Mom and Grandpa Ralph, pulled onto the small dirt cottage road and slowly drove away. When I turned onto Regal Road, I saw a huge crow sitting in the middle of the road. At first, I thought it might be a raven due to its size. I looked more closely at the beak, and realized it was just a big ass crow. I slowed my car to a crawl, hoping to gently nudge him along and give him the hint to move aside. As I got closer to the crow, he didn't budge at all.

"*Ok, then,*" I thought, "*I'm not in a rush to leave, so I'll just be patient and wait.*" Well, it seemed like forever sitting there on that dirt road. No other cars came by. I'm sure it was a ten-minute wait as he just stood there, his body facing westward and looking straight ahead into the bush. Once in a while, he would turn his head and look at me. I recall the dark piercing eyes looking into my soul. He was trying to tell me something, but I wasn't listening. I could have honked my horn to try to get him to move, but I didn't think of it at the time. I was mesmerized by his stature and stillness. We were the only ones on the dirt road, so I just sat there and waited. The crow finally took one small step, then slowly another and another. By then I was getting impatient and was glad to see he was moving, albeit very slowly. When he'd moved over just enough for me to squeeze by, I drove around him and headed for Nana's house, and didn't give the crow another thought.

When we arrived at Nana's home, it was already dark and wintery outside, but the house was warm, inviting, and full of laughter. The cousins were having a blast and the adults were enjoying festive after-dinner conversation at the dinner table.

"*Ok,*" I said to myself, "*it's really time to leave. If I make good time, I will get home by midnight, unpack, prep for work, and launch into a Monday morning routine.*" I really didn't want to leave such bliss and I clearly remember thinking, "*I wish I could stay*" and "*I wish I didn't* **have to** *get home for work.*" But I said my goodbyes one more time and off we went. The weather wasn't too bad – an average snowy drive for a North Bay winter. Sam and I were listening to Simon and Garfunkel on the CD player. She kicked off her boots and coat, snuggled in, and fell asleep somewhere around Powassan.

Though it was really dark on the two-lane highway, there wasn't much traffic. I was driving for the conditions. I had driven that road in winter so many times and winter drives didn't make me nervous at all. But as I came around a bend, I hit black ice. My car spun out of control, sliding across the middle line into the oncoming lane, and heading straight for a rock cut on the other side of the road.

With zero control of my car, my first and most immediate thought was, "*Here we go. This is it.*" An immense sense of peace flooded my body and mind. I had no fear at all, just complete and utter surrender. I actually took my hands off the steering wheel. Time slowed down completely. The thoughts running through my mind slowed down, too. They became crystal clear. I honestly have to say, I had no other awareness than, *"This is it. This is the end."* And I was completely okay with it. I wasn't thinking of the impending approach of the oncoming cars, or the rock cut that I was heading directly towards. Surprisingly, the idea of the eventual crash and collateral damage or injury, and knowing that my precious daughter was in the seat right beside me, was not running through my mind at all. I wasn't thinking of my family, work, or anything in the future. It was like I was in a suspended zone where there was no time, no future, no past. I remember it like it was yesterday. A feeling of pure surrender came over me. I was held in a bubble of suspended time. There was no fear, no worries, just peace.

I'm pretty sure my soul had left my body before the impact because I don't remember hearing or feeling any of it. The angels quickly ushered me to the celestial realms. The next thing I experienced was being instantly transported to a place which I will do my best to describe with human words. I was in a space of **Pure Divine Light**. I did not see the pearly gates or relatives (like others have experienced or which have been depicted in the movies). My NDE played out in stages or layers of awareness. It was a full sensory experience for me and I will do my best to describe it for you in its pure form.

The layers were as such: my impressions were a **feeling**, then **seeing**, then **hearing** – in that order. My first layer of feeling was like that of a child overcome with wonder and awe. I thought, *"Wow, this place is so beautiful and peaceful."* It felt like I was still alive and breathing even though I didn't have a physical body here. The air actually had texture to it. It was as if the energy I was bathed in had a density to it – kind of like what being bathed in liquid light might feel like. I had no awareness of my physical body anymore. I was not a separate or an individuated light body either. Instead, I was literally part of a unified field of light energy that felt like Pure Divine Love. I was part of a whole consciousness. I was not concerned about anything. I had no fear. I was completely detached from the crash that was happening simultaneously in another dimension. My only experience was that of being immersed in a field of Pure Unconditional Love. This feeling of being pure light and energy was exquisite.

Then a second layer of realization came forth. I began to see what was around me. I realized that the space I was in had colour to it – a delicate mixture of incredible pastel pinks, with some incandescent aspects of light blue, purple, silver, and lots of gold. I remember thinking, *"I must be in the presence of Heaven."* I remember trying to look down for my body to see my legs or torso, but all I saw was various colours of light, and I was it! My essence was mingled with everything around me, all the energies were connected, nothing was separate. This was the most incredible feeling. I felt like I was connected to a living entity of universal love. I couldn't have conceived that such a beautiful and safe place ever existed. The space or place or time I found myself in felt expansive – so big, yet perfectly comfortable. I felt the frequencies of colour throughout my being. There was nothing to fear at all. To call this home would be an understatement.

The third sensory experience I had was auditory. I slowly became aware of a subtle sound. In fact, I was vibrating with this sound. It was all around me and through me. It was soft and barely detectable, but as I adjusted to the surroundings, I heard what you might call heavenly music. But, not really. It was more like frequencies, which were so pleasing and reassuring. The most beautiful compilations of musical notes I've heard on Earth couldn't come close to this sound of pure love and joy. Otherworldly for sure, and unforgettable.

Then I remember thinking, *"What is this and where am I*?" However, it was funny that I was "thinking" because I didn't have a head to think with. I was just pure light and energy floating around. I felt so connected to everything. The expanse around me and beyond was vast. Any thoughts or questions were never verbally spoken, yet ideas and answers came to me as an instant knowing. It's as if I was part of the collective heart and mind of God, Spirit, Creation, the Angels, Consciousness…call it whatever you're comfortable with, but it was Divine. It was everything and all things. This is what it felt like to be held in Unconditional Love. There was no judgment here. I was accepted into the fold with loving arms, as it were. I was perfect and Divine and part of a bigger tapestry of consciousness. My explanation just can't do it justice. As I write these words I am instantly transported to the feeling once again. Oh, if only we could all know this feeling, just for once.

The last layer of experience I remember having in Heaven was being aware of some energy presences beside and behind me. I felt them as angelic energies. They were clearly there to hold me in Pure Grace and Pure Love, in support of my journey. At this point, I recall feeling, ***"I am finally home. What a relief."*** I wanted to celebrate and stay. But that was not to be the case at this time. In the very next moment, I was whisked back to the 3rd dimension. I very clearly remember being squeezed back into my body. I use the word squeezed, because it felt like a very tight and uncomfortable fit to get back into my body.

What had felt like a long time in Heaven was only a few seconds in the human world. As soon as I was thrust back into my body, I realized that I'd entered the crash timeline just a few moments after where I'd exited. The car had miraculously missed the rock cut and hit the ditch, catapulted up the hill some distance, and now we were rolling over and over down the embankment. I could feel my head hitting the ground on each roll because the roof of the Sidekick had popped right off and the protective roll-bar had collapsed. I could hear metal and plastic crashing all around me as I was tossed around like a rag doll. I wasn't in any pain though. Yet. I distinctly remember thinking, *"Oh no, I'm back in my body again!"* I couldn't help but feel dread and disappointment, thinking, *"Here we go again. Back for another rodeo ride of life."*

The Aftermath: Picking Up the Pieces

The car finally stopped rolling. Everything was quiet, dark, and still. I opened my eyes and found myself hanging upside down. The car had landed in the ditch at the bottom of the incline. Once I got oriented, I looked over for Samantha. When the car initially spun out, she'd been completely asleep, reclined in her seat. There she was, also hanging upside down, and held in place by her seatbelt. She appeared to be unharmed, but she was stunned and not speaking. I unhooked my seat belt, dropped into the snow, and crawled around to her side of the car. Remaining remarkably calm and talking to her the whole time to reassure her, I reached in and unbuckled her seat belt. She had no shoes or coat on because she took them off to cozy down for a long car ride. Now we found ourselves in a dark, cold, unimaginable situation. I sat on the snowbank and snuggled her on my lap, wrapping her into my coat and taking a moment to gather my wits about me.

Then I heard and saw a frantic woman running towards us. She kept asking me if there was anyone else in the car. I kept replying "No, just us," but she wasn't hearing me. She was hysterical. I guess what she'd just witnessed was pretty scary. I stood up and said, *"Can we please sit in your car?"* That seemed to snap her out of it.

"Oh yes, of course!" she said, and helped us out of the ditch and into her warm car. I began to feel the back of my head and neck starting to swell and get stiff. *"Oh dear,"* I thought to myself, *"I've injured my neck."* I'd had the wherewithal to fill my scarf with snow and use it like an ice pack. The cold soothed my neck. I started feeling like I was fully back in my body (unpleasant as it was to be there again) and so gratefully amazed that, miraculously, Samantha was okay, and unharmed. But she was in shock, and still hadn't uttered a word.

In the aftermath of the crash, the police and ambulance arrived. We were taken into the ambulance and checked over. The nice attendant gave Sam a teddy bear, which she clutched onto for comfort. To this day, when I ask her about her memory of the crash, this is the only thing she recalls – the teddy bear. Not remembering the crash or aftermath was a good thing. I'm sure this was her spiritual protective reflex kicking in on her behalf.

I had fully expected to be taken to the hospital. My neck and head were beginning to hurt and throb, and I was starting to feel foggy in my thinking. But my clinical brain was on duty. I was trying to triage myself and the situation. I recall thinking that the attendant wasn't being very perceptive about my potential injuries.

Because our injuries on the roadside seemed minor to the paramedics on duty that night, and I suppose because I came across as being so calm and collected, we were deemed "just fine." A police car would take us to the station where family could pick us up. Looking back now, I see this was a necessary triage decision they had to make in the midst of chaos and uncertainty, but I couldn't believe we weren't taken to the closest hospital by someone.

Despite the hustle and bustle of emergency workers all around us, I kept the focus on my daughter and myself. When a police officer came and asked for my license and ownership of the car, I burst out laughing and said, *"Ha! If you can find it, it's yours!"* The look on his face told me he was not impressed by my comment, nor thought it was funny. But the whole damn roof of the Sidekick had come off, for God's sake. Our belongings were strewn all over the highway, or buried in the snow somewhere.

They collected what they could find in the dark, loaded us and our stuff into a police car, and drove us to the Burk's Falls police station. On the way, the officer, as kindly as he could, told us that eleven other cars had hit black ice and crashed. They also needed immediate attention. Burk's Falls, being a small northern town, had only one ambulance and a few police cars. Samantha and I, and our pile of belongings, were dropped off in the front vestibule of the station and guided to wait there for our family to arrive. We had no other choice. Since we 'seemed' fine – ambulatory and conscious – they did what they had to do.

My headache soon rolled into a massive migraine. I didn't have any anti-inflammatories or pain killers on me. The vestibule had no heat at all, and as the hours ticked by waiting for Mom and Ralph to arrive, the cold seeped into me and I started to shake. My neck was stiffening up from the severe whiplash. I couldn't think clearly. With no other adults around, I felt alone and vulnerable. I knew I had to dig deep for inner strength and hold it together for Samantha's sake. I did my best to comfort her while keeping myself calm and centered. I kept a good eye on her, physically checking her out once in a while. She seemed fine, but she still wasn't speaking. I knew she was in shock and who could blame her? She went to sleep cozy in the car and awoke upside down in a cold, dark snow bank.

Then suddenly, I remembered that in my luggage I had some Rescue Remedy (a Bach flower essence for shock and trauma). I dug around in my make-up bag and fished it out. I was very surprised it wasn't lost in the roll-over because everything was all over the highway. I silently thanked the officer who went through all the trouble of gathering my stuff, and squirted some Rescue Remedy into Samantha's mouth. Within seconds, she was cheerfully talking up a storm. What a relief to hear her jabbering away. That was indeed one **Holy Roll**. Not a scratch on her and no physical trauma. I am amazed her body wasn't thrown from the vehicle. The seatbelt, and no doubt her Angels, had held her in place through all of it. I'll say it again: it was truly a miracle.

Three long hours later I saw the headlights of mom's car roll up to the station doors. I still couldn't believe we'd been abandoned by the police and unattended all that time. I'd felt so alone, and had to dig deep for inner strength, holding it together for Samantha's sake. As soon as my mom opened the door, I broke down and cried like a baby. With another capable adult there to take the lead, all the stress came pouring out of me. I passed her the proverbial baton and let go.

The next four to five days were a blur. When we arrived back in North Bay, I ran down the medical signs and symptoms for my mother to watch for, and then I surrendered to rest and recuperation. My mother midwifed me back into my body and started the healing process. For days, she attended to me at the bedside while also taking care of Samantha. I am sure Mom was dosing me with appropriate homeopathic remedies, and applying lotions and potions to my wounds. In some of my lucid moments, I could feel her giving me Therapeutic Touch. I knew all was well in her loving and very capable hands.

When I was well enough to drive back to Waterloo and pick up the pieces of my life, I was still running in what I call "work" mode, or 3D mode. With all the work and life obligations waiting for me, I didn't give myself space to fully unpack the whole emotional experience – the crow spirit, the crash, and the NDE. Self-inquiry and curiosity took a back seat to my other responsibilities and earthly preoccupations. For example, on the drive home I was oddly obsessed with going by the car wrecker's to see my vehicle and retrieve the CD in the player. I could still remember the song that was playing when I crashed. It was Simon and Garfunkel's "Homeward Bound" (the irony of this song title is not lost on me). I wanted my CD back. I was focused on material items at a time when I had just had a brush with death! And I was stressed over how to reschedule the patients that were canceled and how much work it would be to make up the clinical time. These kinds of things were rolling around in my head. I still hadn't connected the dots of what crow spirit was trying to tell me that day. I'll never forget that auspicious experience. But I pushed it to the back of my brain. I got on with life, and tried to heal physically from the crash.

Chapter Two

The Road Home to Wholeness and Healing

When I finally returned home, I was grateful and keenly aware of how fortunate it was that I worked with three talented chiropractors. They were always available to treat my neck and head injuries. How could it get any better than that!

During a treatment on my first day back, Dr. Ward asked, "Dawn, are you aware that there is grass embedded in your scalp?" *"Are you kidding me?"* I answered. I couldn't believe that, through all that snow and after several hair washings, my head had repeatedly hit the ground so hard that grass was embedded into my skin. It's truly a miracle that I survived. I should have had a broken neck. Imagine it like this: the torsion and impact of the roll-over was like taking the head of a mushroom and twisting it off. My head should have popped off, but it didn't. I obviously still had a purpose in this lifetime to play out. It wasn't my 'time'. But I was left with severe whiplash, ligament instability, expanded skull bones and concussion issues that would haunt me for years to come.

I was alive, but some days I wished otherwise. It would have been so much easier just to stay on the other side of the veil. Once you get a glimpse of Heaven and an awareness of the formless glory of your spiritual existence, it can be hard to adapt to and accept the conditions of our human lives. Despite my ongoing discomfort, I was thankful for all the physical assistance my chiropractor friends offered me. I can't tell you how many thousands of treatments I had over the years. Some mornings, I couldn't get out of bed and Dr. Ken would make house calls. Dr. Ward would come over after a long day's work to give me an adjustment, too. I couldn't sleep through even one night without pain, minor or severe, and as a result I was worn out and sleep deprived for what seemed like a lifetime.

I soon ended up married to one of those chiropractors. (How amazing was that?) Dr. Ward and I had three beautiful children together and each had one daughter from previous relationships. The next 20 or so years I was blessed with this beautiful family, and a supportive and loving husband. Life was full, and busy. Raising a family was my joy, and somehow, I found time to run a clinic and serve as a Naturopathic Doctor full time as well.

Looking back, I remember so many moments of love and joy. But it was always over-shadowed by the ongoing pain and inflammation of the injuries from the car crash. I was functional enough most days, so many people couldn't tell I was struggling. Then there were days when I was incapacitated and couldn't even hold my babies or nurse them without assistance. The majority of my days and nights, I struggled with relentless chronic pain. As a Naturopathic Doctor you can imagine I tried many natural remedies to assist me with the pain. However, occasionally, I resorted to pain medication just to get a good night's sleep.

As time marched on, I was getting worn out. Without a restorative night's sleep, my body struggled to heal. Many days I lost my emotional resiliency completely and came undone. I did my best to hold it together, but my marriage began to suffer. Sometimes all it would take was a roll-over in bed, or pulling a sweater over my head, and my neck would give out; I would be in so much pain and spasm that I couldn't get out of bed. I would miss days of work. I felt like a wreck and my emotional strength was wearing thin.

Thank God I married a chiropractor though. My husband was always supportive and helpful. He was my angel on duty literally 24/7. Many nights I would wake him up because I was in so much pain that I couldn't sleep. I always felt so badly waking him up from his much-needed rest. And he always helped me out – sometimes with one eye open – but his heart was always in it. Ward was forever patiently putting me back together and this became my normal. Every time I aggravated my neck,

I would ask for help again, and was so grateful for his support. Just when I thought I was turning a corner and I felt almost 'normal', I would get worse again, and around and around I would go.

Being in the natural and alternative field of medicine I had many rehabilitation options available for my neck, head, and nervous system. I explored every unique and different chiropractic technique available. I also tried acupuncture, osteopathy, craniosacral therapy, and neuro-therapy. You name it, I gave it a go. The relief would last hours or days, but nothing was "healing" me in any permanent or sustainable way. I spent years chasing a physical cure.

Looking back, I realize I had the narrow focus of just wanting to be out of pain. I focused on fixing the structure only, reducing my body to parts of a machine. Apparently, I was barking up the wrong tree for true, sustainable healing. I wasn't seeing past the physical injuries and being curious of their roots – the emotional and spiritual aspects. I wasn't asking questions like:

> *"Why did this happen in the first place?"*
> *"What needs to be seen here?"*
> *"What is my body trying to tell me?"*
> *"What do I need right now to heal?"*
> *"What is the meaning behind all of this?"*

I wasn't approaching my situation from a truly holistic vantage point at all. In fact, I was completely neglecting the spiritual meaning behind the whole "accident" (that wasn't an "accident" in the first place). I was busy running a household and a business. I guess my wisdom years hadn't kicked in yet. I had not fully awakened to the possibility of deeper meanings of injury or illness, and I still had a lot to learn. I felt I had a very spiritually centered life, mind you. My relationship with God was strong and I had explored and lived many facets of religion, spirituality, and metaphysical and mystical experiences. Yet I still hadn't connected the dots and the meaning of what was happening to me. It was coming; divine timing was unfolding, albeit slowly. I had to follow the trail of breadcrumbs.

I was mostly hopeful of a recovery, yet sometimes I couldn't help falling into disappointment and despair. I wondered, *"Would I ever be without pain again? Other people seem to get better, why not me? What did I do to deserve this?"* I had all these questions, and no answers were presenting themselves – yet.

Coming Full Circle: Following the Mystical Path

Let's fast forward to Christmas of 2018. By this time, Samantha was all grown up and living in Australia with a family of her own. She had barely any memory of the crash, and it left no lasting impression on her.

I still had three children, either living at home or at university close by. Life was chugging along. Two weeks before Christmas, I started feeling very unwell. Oh dear. I felt like the base of my skull had been smashed with a wooden 2 x 4, right where my head would have hit the ground during the roll-overs of the crash. It seemed to come out of nowhere. I hadn't been this bad off since the aftermath of the crash. It felt like the original injury flared up again in full force. It was like the initial injury imprint resurfaced. My head was swollen, my neck was swollen, my brain felt bruised, my head was pulsing. Something felt very wrong. I worried that it might be an aneurysm bursting, or a cerebral vascular event finally catching up with me from the initial trauma. I immediately consulted my usual practitioners. They were concerned as well, and suggested it would be best to get a head CT scan or at least get checked out at the hospital. You would think, being a doctor myself and of sound mind, I would have followed their advice, right? Wrong. Something within me – a deep feeling I couldn't quite explain – deterred me from going to the hospital. It truly was the strangest and most frightening experience. I alternated back and forth between, *"Go to the hospital, Dawn,"* and this voice in my head that kept saying, *"No, you don't need to, you'll be fine."* At this point you may jump to the conclusion that I was a fool, or maybe having a delusional experience. But hang on, let me finish the amazing story.

Christmas Day arrived and I still felt unwell. We'd been invited to my brother's place for Christmas dinner, which was an hour and a half drive towards the Toronto area. I contemplated the options of what to do and where to go over Christmas, and considered just staying home in bed to rest. Then I heard the voice in my head again. *"Go to Christmas dinner and continue driving to North Bay that evening."*

Though I thought this was a crazy idea considering my condition, and was concerned about leaving home and my support system, I heard and felt this with every fiber of my being. A strong knowing dropped into me. I pushed my concerns aside and I listened. I wasn't even in control of my actions at this point. My Higher Self took the reins, giving me clear directions. My oldest son Michael and I packed up and got ready to leave. He had just gotten his driver's license and had no highway driving experience. Yet, off we went. I loaded up on Advil to manage the pain and inflammation because it was the only thing working at this point. I gave the car keys to Michael and said, *"Get us to Uncle Dave's place for Christmas dinner and then we will drive to North Bay later that evening."* He agreed, and was very happy to go visit North Bay and family.

We had a lovely Christmas gathering with my brother and family. I decided to cut our visit short only because I wanted to get to North Bay before midnight if we could. It was a 3-hour drive from his house, on dark, snowy roads. I had faith in Michael. He was a very safe driver, albeit inexperienced. So, I settled in with a pillow in the passenger's seat, made myself as comfortable as possible, and away we went. I'd forgotten that on Christmas Eve many of the rest stops along the way would be closed, but that was okay. We had a full tank of gas and our stomachs were full of turkey. I must have nodded off about half way there. Michael woke me up asking if I could take over the driving.

"Oh man, I am in no shape to drive, Mike." I begged him to keep going, and told him he was doing a great job, but he insisted we switch up. He was feeling uncomfortable and really wanted a break.

"Okay then, Michael. When you feel it's safe, find a place to pull over and we can switch up." In the dark, it was hard to see the upcoming turn offs and rest stops until we were virtually on top of them. Since it wasn't safe to make a quick turn on the snowy roads, Michael just kept on sailing past them. He was too nervous to make a sharp turn in dark, unfamiliar territory. One

option after another came and went. I could tell he was getting frustrated.

"Don't worry, Michael. I trust you. When you feel safe, pull over and I will drive. Take your time," I said, and closed my eyes again to rest. I was fighting the pain and not looking forward to driving the rest of the way.

Finally, I felt the car slow down and pull off the main highway. The off-ramp took us onto a side road and Michael pulled into a 'random' parking lot. I sat up from my reclined position and couldn't believe my eyes. Michael had pulled into the parking lot of the police station in Burk's Falls. I found myself staring right at the exact place where Samantha and I had been dropped off the night of the crash. With the headlights shining into the front vestibule, the whole memory of being there came flooding back to me. I honestly couldn't believe it. Michael was not even born when the roll-over crash happened and didn't know much about it at all. He especially didn't know about the Burk's Falls police station. Yet somehow, this is where he chose to pull off – lead by Spirit no doubt.

Holy Moly. The Mystical Journey was rolling out in Divine order. In a state of suspended animation, I stepped out of the car and told him what this place meant to me. He started to giggle. I remember the slight smile he had on his face, as if he was glad to have picked the right spot. I was beginning to understand the purpose behind this crazy adventure back up North. Wow, you can't make this stuff up.

I stared at the station entrance and immediately, I felt instructions download into me. The voice said, *"Unpack everything and leave it here."* I knew what this meant. Energetically, through the power of my imagination (psychic intuition), I took a suitcase, opened it up, and moved the energetic charge of all my traumatic memories into that container. I brought out every last bit of emotion and left it there. I let it go. It took some time. With my eyes closed, I purged all of the pain, fear, concern, and disappointments, dumping them into the energetic suitcase. Then I closed it and left it at the door of the police station. In doing so, I had transmuted the energetic imprint that this place still held for me. On this mystical path to healing I had to physically return to the crash site, and this was the closest I could get to it. The original highway where I had my NDE was no longer in use. A new bypass had been built. Nevertheless, it was done. I felt lighter and reassured in my heart.

This trip wasn't just a journey home. This was a pilgrimage, and a critical piece on my road to healing. Literally, I was coming full circle. The miracle in all of this was that Michael and I played our parts in this retracing quite easily and willingly. I continued to let my Spirit (Higher Self) guide me. You perhaps could think of this journey as a spiritual treasure hunt. I followed the nudges, the clues, the downloads, the feelings, and the voices that availed themselves to me. I surrendered and followed the trail of breadcrumbs. I knew I was on my road back to wholeness – to healing – but I didn't even realize the extent of it yet.

We both got back in the car and continued our trip to North Bay, arriving safely to my uncle and aunt's home on the lake. It was just up the road from my mother's home, which we sold after her passing in 2006. (More about that later.) Physically, I still didn't feel well, and emotionally, I felt vulnerable, but I was trusting the process. We had a quiet, restful visit with the family. I chose to spend a lot of time in meditation. I was aware that this amazing process was unfolding. I wanted to understand it and fully surrender to it. But this puzzle still had a missing piece.

The day before we were to return to our home in Stratford, Ontario, I felt the impulse to call my beloved teacher and healer, Janet Sinclair. She is known as the Urban Shaman in our area. She is a gift to the world, and a powerful healer. Janet had been assisting me on my road to mastery in traditional healing ways. Who and what Janet embodied, and how she worked, were both familiar and fascinating to me. I knew I was in good hands. Our earlier sessions together called out parts of me – aspects of past lives and skills needed in this life stream. It was no accident that we'd been introduced and were working together at this time in my life. Something in me knew she was going to help me to heal the last bits. Spirit would show me, through her, what was needed for my body, mind, and spirit to heal from the original traumatic event.

Spirit continued to line up all these synchronistic opportunities and events. Janet had a busy schedule, as did I. I felt a real need to meet with her, but how on earth could we pull it off before I'd have to go back to work? As the universe would have it, she immediately said, "If you're coming back Sunday, come see me in the evening for a healing session and we will see what we can conjure up."

Sunday evening, I arrived at Janet's place and we proceeded into sacred space for a ceremony of shamanic healing. I felt so held in love and safety with her. As we danced and flowed in the magical energy, time expanded and contracted until there was no sense of time at all. Three hours seemed like one. Janet invited her guides and healing team, as did I, and we surrendered to Spirit. The Reiki energy (universal life force healing energy) was flying that night. When she placed her hands at the back of my head and neck, the pain intensified. I trusted that the energy was working itself out, opening the blockages and letting in a healing matrix that was needed to correct the damage. This is what I now understand and call 'healing in the original imprint.' Indeed, this is what was happening. Janet had tapped into the NDE experience on the other side. She clearly saw and explained this to me:

"Dawn, this was your potential exit point. You did indeed leave your body and were on the other side of the veil. You didn't want to return. There was some resistance. But at that moment, you chose to rewrite your contract and enter back into your body to be with your daughter Samantha. You vowed to be there for her and not to leave her at this time."

I think I cried at this moment, out of sheer joy. I knew this was a love so deep and this was not the first life stream with Samantha. In fact, Samantha, my mother, and I share a very special bond. The three of us have had many lives together. We were all mothers or daughters to each other at different times. In this lifetime, sometimes these lines blurred, leaving our roles in a big jumble, but together we shared experiences and wisdom in amazing ways. We had more work to do together in this life for sure.

By the end of the healing session, I was exhausted but so grateful for Janet and the helpful spirits who assisted. I got up from the table feeling spinny, which is usual, but solid at the same time, and grounded in my body. I left with such appreciation and infinite love for Janet's help. I spent the next few days integrating all of it. I felt really good and very pleased. The throbbing and mental fogginess from my head and neck pain had cleared. I wondered, *"Is this it? Is my healing complete?"*

As the days, weeks, and months progressed, my physical body felt stronger than it had since the injury. I could sleep for the first time in decades without pain! I could roll over and not have to be careful of every angle of my head, the slope of the pillow, the speed of movement. *"Was this what it was like to be normal?"* I wondered.

The following summer I was still feeling pretty damn good. Only occasionally would I feel the need to get a chiropractic adjustment to tweak things back into alignment. But it was minimal compared to what was needed previously. I was going for adjustments for "normal" stuff now. Dr. Orr, one of my chiropractors, said to me (and I laugh every time I think of this), "Your C1 vertebrae is no longer in another postal code, Dawn. Whatever you've done, I am happy for you." On many occasions after the crash, Ward had mentioned that he'd never felt a neck quite like mine. He noticed the improvement, too. Regardless of their assessments, I knew I was feeling better. I was even able to return to diving into the swimming pool, which in the past would have debilitated me for a week. Not anymore.

I was overjoyed. I had finally released the pattern of pain and trauma. Christmas 2018 had appeared to be an extreme exacerbation of the neck and head trauma – maybe even a potential vascular crisis – but turned out to be **the Divine road home to healing and wholeness**. If I would have gone into fear and not listened to the dictates of my higher Soul Self, I would have missed this miraculous opportunity – my mystical healing. Trusting my higher guidance was the key for me. I had the courage to listen to my heart, not my head, where reactions and responses are programmed into my subconscious. Emerging from this experience highlighted what I have always known about human emotional and mental reasoning. We are a collection of generational experiences, whose programs have kept us in fear, and kept us from knowing the innate power of our wisdom and healing capacity. Entertaining the idea that a traumatic event could possibly serve us in healing ways was now on the table for me. Self-responsibility and self-inquiry are ways we are not usually accustomed to, but it was the ticket for me. Having gone through this journey has humbled me and expanded my understanding of the intricate and miraculous capabilities of the body, mind, and spirit. We are Divine in nature, and I invite you to explore your potential, my friend.

Chapter Three

A Little Bit About Spirit Animals, Guides & Totems

Many cultures, especially indigenous cultures, recognize the mystical relationships we have with spirit animals. For them, animals are said to hold special and deep meaning in the spirit worlds. Spirit animals are often described as a 'family of belonging we have in the animal world' or a 'spiritual kinship' we have with them. A spirit animal is one that best matches our vibe or mirrors our inborn traits, purpose, strengths, and weaknesses. Some cultures make a distinction between animal guides and totems. An animal totem is described as your protector or helper – one that will show up in your life when you need it. Whether you are speaking of an animal spirit or totem, they are all helpers that support us. They come into and out of our lives as companions to teach us, guide us, protect us, or assist us in unique and specific ways. Aboriginal cultures have ceremonies where they call in or connect with their particular spirit animal, totem, or tribe. In doing so, they open their awareness to the 'medicine' which that animal offers, and incorporate it into their lives. Once the spirit or totem animal is discovered, they walk closely with that spirit animal and spend their whole lives mastering the medicine. This is a precious and revered relationship.

Some spirit animals can show up in your dreams, in your backyard, on a camping trip, on a dream quest, on a billboard, or on the road, like mine did. That crow was my animal spirit guide and totem and was trying to get my attention in order to protect me. How do I know this? Allow me to explain.

Crow: My Spirit Guide and Totem

When I was a new, young Naturopathic Doctor, my very first patient became my teacher. His name was Daniel Blasutti, and he was a blessing to anyone who had the privilege of knowing him. A very successful business man in his younger years, Daniel found himself facing his own demise and mortality when he was diagnosed with cancer. He immediately quit his corporate job and decided to explore what life still had to offer him, while enjoying the time he had left with his family and friends.

Daniel was more than a patient; we became close friends. He shared a wise insight one day with me. He realized he had spent his whole life climbing the proverbial corporate ladder, only to realize in the end "it was leaning up against the wrong building". I'll never forget him telling me these words. He was basically saying that success, as most of the world knows it, was all wrong. It isn't the material wealth that we work so hard to accumulate, or the accolades we receive when we accomplish great things, that are truly important. Success, he was saying, "is the health of our spiritual life and the depth of relationships we have." That was the greatest life lesson he wanted everyone to know about. He was bursting with insights in his last days.

One day I was on a home visit with him, since he was so weak and couldn't leave his house. I would usually find him in his art studio making sculptures, his oxygen tube following him around as he puttered. He finally had time to realize the passions he had inside of him, and he wanted to spend his last days doing what he loved. That day I found him finishing a beautiful sketch of a woman who had a crow artistically entangled in her dark hair. He was a wonderful artist, and I found this picture particularly mesmerizing. I could feel the energy emerging from the picture, and asked, "Who is the woman in the picture?" I will never forget his answer. He said, **"This is you. You are Crow Woman. You help people cross over."** His words landed like a lead balloon. I gulped and felt a great weight of responsibility instantly come upon me. I wouldn't know how poignant this was until much later in life.

I went home that night and immediately looked up the spiritual meaning of the crow. Google didn't exist yet, but I had an animal spirit book (the name of which I've forgotten). I wrote the passage in my journal:

> *"Crows are symbolic of change, transition, and metamorphosis. They have psychic insight and they can shift one's spiritual or emotional well-being. Crows are the bird that mediate between life and death. Natives understood that the crow is a carrion bird that actually embodies death."*

Then I read that *"**crows often show up and remind you to pay attention to the spiritual messages that are sent to guide you.**"*

Oh My God. It is no coincidence that a crow showed up to give me a spiritual message the night of the crash, trying to stop me from driving home. That very night, I did experience death and rebirth. I was in between life and death, which was both a Divine gift and a hardship. Daniel had foreshadowed aspects of my life that I had yet to integrate and understand. *"Thank you, Daniel, my incredible friend and teacher. I miss you."*

In Shamanism, the act of dying is said to be the most heightened spiritual level you can experience. It represents death of the ego and remembrance of your highest essence, which is Pure Spirit. They believe, at the time of death, you experience the ending and separation of one state of being, the physical body, that then leads to a higher spiritual existence – pure energy, where you exist as a Spirit of light and love. I was able to experience both states that night, crossing over and coming back. It was the first time I had full and complete awareness of my true existence as Spirit and knew my physical embodiment was temporary and fleeting in the grand scheme of my soul's journey.

My NDE served as a gateway and the beginning of a spiritual awakening on a whole new level. Since then, my spiritual connection to crows has grown and blossomed in ways I couldn't have imagined. Over the years I have forged great respect for crow, becoming more familiar with its medicine day by day. I absolutely love the cawing sound and the deep dark black colour of crow feathers. Their mystical powers intrigue me. When they fly towards me, swooping closely overhead within a few feet, I feel an incredible energy of blessing coming straight into me. This bird has such meaning for me now. I always listen to the messages of the crow and I never take them for granted anymore. I have developed the ability to hear and communicate with them on many levels. Naturally, after the crash warning, they have become my totems for traveling and driving. I call them my travel buddies. We have developed a communication system which is very helpful and meaningful for me. For example, while I'm driving, if a crow flies beside me on the right-hand side, that means *the way is all clear and good*. If the crow crosses in front of my car from left to right, it's an immediate warning to *take notice, be careful and slow down*. If I pass crows sitting on the side of the road, it's a reminder that *they are here for me, they are saying hello and all is well*. Sometimes when I see them sitting alongside the road, a very specific message that I need at the time drops right into my consciousness. We have developed clairaudient communication. For instance, once I had a crow fly over my car. It approached from behind, swooping down over the front windshield and then holding itself there, traveling at the same speed of my car. The message I received was, *full speed ahead, get there quickly, I will clear the way*. As chance would have it, I was needed urgently where I was headed.

"My" crows are not just for travel insights; they help me in other ways as well. For instance, when I find myself wondering if I am on the right track, or if I'm doubting that what I am doing is making a difference, *or wondering if something is the right thing, or right timing*, a crow will almost immediately perch itself on the centre and highest point of a nearby tree, and begin cawing loudly to get my attention. The message is, "Hey, we are here with you. You are in truth and alignment. Keep going." This often happens while I am walking from my clinic parking lot towards the office on days when I know that my case load will be complicated and challenging. The crows are always there supporting, inspiring, and nudging me on. I am grateful to have cultivated such a magical relationship with them.

Crows are also said to have insight into unseen realms. Others say that crows are supernatural creatures and can communicate with humans. Crows do feel supernatural to me, and my connection with crow spirit over the years has never let me down. I have even played around with remote viewing through crow's eyes – a phenomenal experience. I always honour and listen to these helpful and compassionate animal spirits now that I understand their role in my life.

My Lesson from Spirit

"Betrayal of yourself is the highest betrayal of all."
Neale Donald Walsch

I wasn't always connected to my spirit guides like I am now. I realize, looking back at life, that my guides and helpers were always with me. But I wasn't always aware and listening to them in my younger years. There is an important lesson the crow spirit was trying to teach me the night of the car crash that I would like to share with you. But first, notice I avoid saying the word car "accident" when referring to the crash. It is because it was not "accidental" at all and this will become apparent as you follow along. If you recall, earlier in the book I referred to the younger days of my career when I was so busy taking care of everyone else, putting everyone else's needs first, and letting obligation and responsibility be my leading edge. I admit to being that person, for sure, and some days I still default to this mode of operation. That kind of living was a big fat program – a program I learned very well from well-intentioned and loving parents. Mom and Dad were both Type-A workaholics (that's where I get my hard work ethic from). At the same time, they were so gracious and generous, always putting others' needs before their own and working hard at their own expense. I saw this in action and – surprise – it rubbed off on me. This is human nature.

We all learn patterns of behavior and absorb values and belief systems from our most influential caregivers, usually our parents and close family members. This is how human beings are designed. An infant and child's brain is one big downloadable computer. Psychologists have determined that a child's brain from 1-7 years of age is predominantly in a theta state, which is a perfect state for hypnosis. What better way to learn how to survive and navigate your world than to have your brain operate like one big sponge and take in everything you see and witness in your world. It's a perfect set-up for survival of the species, isn't it? When it comes down to it, we are essentially a bundle of reactions and responses that are conditioned into us from a very early age. The down side is we all absorb the programs to which we were exposed; we can't stop it. For instance, I learned to work hard, show up and be responsible, and strive to "do your best at all costs, even if it compromises your health or values." Sound familiar to anyone? We cling to these beliefs and values which sometimes keep us from living from a place of curiosity, love, and growth. Instead, we tend to hang onto our comfortable ways and let fear take the lead. I see this all the time in my clinical practice. Changing programming can be difficult and scary. It is far easier to let the subconscious programming run the show and stay safe, isn't it? Psychologists agree that we become what we believe ourselves to be, and we create our reality from these beliefs, all the way back to our childhood.

The night of the car crash, crow spirit persistently tried to get my attention and stop me from getting on the icy roads. Instead of listening, I was focused on my work responsibilities and not at all open to the message crow had for me. I was running my program and didn't realize it. I was in my head and not in my heart. I was not listening to the dictates and desires of my Higher Self that night. I had put my needs – my longing to stay with family and safety – on the back burner, and instead put the needs of others ahead of mine. My "had to get back to work" program was running the show and that night I had to learn the hard way to listen to and honour myself. **This was a classic case of *betrayal of myself* and I paid a price for it. If I would have tuned into crow's obvious message of, "Stop; don't drive tonight", I would have avoided years of pain and injury. Lesson number one: listen to your heart. Don't betray yourself** in an attempt to please others. Check.

Now, I could have chosen to listen to my Higher Self that night. I could have tapped into my heart and the feelings of my soul. And of course, I could have paid attention to the stand-off with the crow. I didn't, but it is important to point out that I have no regrets. I fully accept and appreciate the choices I made. That night, I chose a path, and it was exactly what I needed to experience. I chose a timeline with specific lessons to learn. After all, out of my experience, this book was born.

We all have free will and we can choose any path we want at any moment. It doesn't make one choice better than another. These are just aspects of life and human experience we need to understand. We really can't get it wrong or right; it's all an experience our souls decide to have. Think of it like choosing a specific book from the library of life, and this is your story you decided to read in this life-time. Granted we may choose easier paths compared to another, but ease and hardship are not important at all. **Our soul chooses what *we need* in order to navigate, learn, evolve, and grow**. When we let go of the right-or-wrong/good-or-bad judgments we put on our life choices, we move into neutrality and surrender. We move out of suffering and pain into joy and gratitude.

As my office administrator often shares:

"Like my mother always said, those who don't listen have to feel."
Wanda Fleming

The above quote can serve as a reminder to tune in and listen to the people and things that are put on your path. If you somehow miss the message life brings to you, you may have a bumpier road to navigate, and Spirit will try again to get your attention in order to encourage change, growth or expansion. **However, no matter what road you take, it will still serve you in a higher, Divine way. Lesson Number Two. Check.**

It's taken me a long time to learn healthy boundaries and balance. And to be honest, even in my 50s, I still have difficulty with boundaries sometimes. These conditioned programs run deep. But now, after many hard lessons on this topic, I notice when I am compromising my well-being with work, other obligations, or in trying to please others. Suffice it to say, I am now open to listening to my Higher Self and receiving assistance from the unseen realms. As I mature and evolve, my relationship with Spirit grows stronger and my boundaries grow healthier.

My advice to you, my friend, is to listen to the nudges from Spirit. The universe is here to teach us all; it's one big school house. Call on your guides for assistance and then watch, listen, and feel the messages. They will come in many different ways, so pay attention.

Over ten years ago, I read a book called Dying to Be Me, by Anita Moorjani. Some of you might know this famous story about her NDE. I loved it from start to finish and I recommend that everyone read it when you are young, and then read it again as you mature. The lessons in the book will land in your heart at different levels of awareness as your life circumstances play out and your levels of maturity and readiness grow. One of the messages that hit home for me (and there are many) was, **"Live your life like your life depends on it, because it does!"** Holy cow, she was right.

Maybe you can avoid a car crash or a seemingly horrible situation in your life if you embody this message that *"betrayal of yourself is the highest betrayal of all."* Maybe not; it's perfect either way. This quote may sound like a harsh or selfish statement, but it really isn't. Here's another way of saying it, in my own words: ***"Honour your needs and desires, and in doing so, remember to listen. Listen to your heart. It will speak to you and guide you always."***

Listening to Spirit and Our Guides

Prior to the car crash, I didn't have the luxury of anyone sharing this wisdom with me. I wish I had. However, my life journey unfolded in the exact and Divine ways I needed. I have embraced and blessed my journey. It has been a powerful teacher.

If you take from this book one thing, please let it be this:

You are never alone; help is always there for you across the veil; reach out, connect, ask for assistance and you'll get it.

Let's first clarify what I mean when I use the word Spirit. Spirit can mean many things, not all of which I will describe here. For the sake of this book, I will be using the word Spirit to describe the Divine, God, Creator, Source, Universal Consciousness, or whatever grand spiritual conductor of life makes sense to you. I also use the term Spirit to describe a consciousness that we are individually connected to, like a guide, who may come into our lives at a particular time to aid us from a higher vibrational state. Spirit guides are extremely helpful. They can offer assistance, protection, support, guidance, and compassion when we need it most. It's likely been happening to you all along and you didn't even notice. Some spirit guides have been with you your entire life. Some drop in when needed, or you can **request their support** as you require it. They come in all forms: animals, pets, angels, departed loved ones, ascended masters, or guardian angels for example. No matter what your culture, religion, or spiritual beliefs, we all have guides in the spiritual worlds working with us for our highest good. It is to our benefit to cultivate a relationship with Spirit, and invite the Divine into our lives.

Humans have free will; this is a spiritual law. Spirit guides can't make decisions for us, do the work for us, or intervene on our behalf without our permission. But they are always there, just waiting for us to ask for assistance. Hey, I am sure each of could use all the help we can get, so let's plug into Spirit and get the signs and nudges to help us along our life path. Open your heart and trust. They will undoubtedly help you take the next best steps for your soul's highest learning and evolution. In the appendix I have a few methods and tools you can explore and have fun with to assist in this process. Be patient with yourself and open your heart. Everything happens in Divine timing.

Your Inner Guidance System

We also have our own inner guidance system. I call this the *"dictates of our soul."* These dictates can be delicate nudges or intense forces. The best way to describe inner guidance is that *unshakable feeling of knowing exactly what you need to do – that strong intuition or gut feeling you can't shake.* It's the kind of situation where you say, **"I don't know why, but I just know I have to do it."** These are some of the ways your soul draws you to the right path or decision in life (the one that serves your highest good). Consider this natural ability your connection to your Higher Self, which is your Soul Self. There is no difference.

I'm sure you've heard this many times and in many different ways before: "Listen to your soul. Let it guide you!" There is so much truth and wisdom in this saying. But who reading this book right now is tuned in and turned onto their inner guidance system? If you are, maybe you don't need this chapter at all, but if you are seeking or struggling to connect to your Higher Self, please read on.

Let's unpack the concept of decision making a little bit. Often in life we give our innate power away and don't even realize it. We let the messages and programs from the outside world influence us too much, and as a result, we make choices *not* for our highest good or *not* from our soul truth. We often comprise our own value systems and do what we think is expected of us instead. We end up making a decision because it's the acceptable thing to do *or* what we were *told* to do. Then once our ego gets in on the act, it can have a field day justifying why we should or should not do something. Sound familiar? Sometimes these externally lead choices can crush us when we later realize we've betrayed our authentic selves or higher truth. Or it could spur us towards personal growth if we are open, ready, and willing. So, my friend, who are you going to listen to? Others' ideas and opinions, or your inner guidance and soul messages? Which road will you take – the road of trust or the road of fear?

These questions are not presented to put pressure on you or judge you in any way. They are asked to get you thinking and to open your awareness about how you live your life. Life will *always* present us with options, opportunities, paths, and choices. We may choose to go left instead of right and experience a very different scenario or outcome.

But it's important to remember that one choice is not better than the other. One is not wrong, and the other right. We are all just having an experience in this human life. We have preferences along the way, and that's perfectly acceptable. I think it's important though to be detached from our outcomes, and instead, revel in the experience. You know the old saying: "It's the journey and not the destination that counts." Whoever said that was right on. The experience is what it's all about. This is how we grow and learn in our humanness. These experiences – every single one of them – are helping our souls to evolve. The end result or outcome of our choices is not as important as how **we chose to be in that situation, what we learned from the situation, and what we became because of the situation.** That is the real gift. How we choose to view the situations in our lives will inevitably shape our outcomes.

So, as we bump along the road of life, we will inevitably experience ups and downs, emotional and otherwise. This is called being human. The stressful or traumatic events, the illnesses, and the people and situations that come into our lives are the dance; this is what we came here for. So, take the pressure off yourself about getting things wrong or right. The good, the bad and the ugly – embrace it all and grow. As St. Francis of Assisi said, "Wear life as a loose garment."

Your soul is here to evolve through human experiences. Sometimes we lose sight of this and get caught up in life drama and struggles. I know – it happens to me too. Having my NDE reminds me, though, that we are an embodied consciousness, a soul that has chosen to come here to experience being human.

> **Being human is not the whole story of who we are.**
> **So, when life gets crazy, remember you are a Divine Soul having this human experience.**

Many of us walk around day to day not realizing this truth. Even though you have a body, a Sacred Body in fact, you are not this body. You are a Spirit of True Love. One of life's important remembrances is that life is happening *for* us, not *to* us. If we keep this in mind when times seem hard and unbearable, it can help us keep perspective. We can hold ourselves in compassion, and love ourselves through the whole enchilada. We are here for a short time in the grand plan of our soul's journey. This human form is just a costume for a short while. The one behind the costume, this one is eternal.

It is a gift to have our human opportunities to grow and evolve. As you find yourself learning and growing in this big cosmic classroom, remember that you have assistance. You are not alone. You are not here by accident. You can always be in touch with Spirit. Know this, trust this. We will explore this concept in much more depth in Chapter Six.

Allow me to share a teaching with you from one of my mentors, Dr. Darren Weissman. It helped me tremendously and may help you as well. Let's consider for a moment a situation that may appear to be tragic or horrible by our usual standards: a young child dying of cancer, an accident that ends in death or a disability, or the loss of one's house in a flood. Dr. Weissman calls these **"gifts in strange wrapping paper."** I love this quote. It's genius, and I live by it. What he means is, all situations are meant for you, divinely crafted for your soul's evolution, and for others in your life who will benefit from the experience. Everyone you connect with – your family, friends, co-workers, therapists, store clerks, contractors, etc. – will also be affected, as they experience life with you or simply witness your journey. Everyone plays a role in the unified tapestry of life. Nothing happens in a vacuum; we are all connected. We are all of service to each other and to everything.

To sum up this chapter:
- We are never alone in this human journey;
- We have all incarnated into these physical bodies for specific soul missions;
- We all create different containers and opportunities for our souls' experiences;
- Everything is happening in our lives for a reason;
- Trust your inner guidance;
- You have preferences along the way, but you can't get it wrong;
- Betrayal to yourself is the highest form of betrayal.

I know you've heard this before and you may think it's a bunch of bogus positive thinking stuff. But I assure you, it is the truth. As humans, we have very limited insight into the spiritual dimensions. These intricate connections are also known as collective consciousness, the quantum field, or source field of information. Some people are more aware than others regarding the nature of the quantum universe and all its workings. Some are plugged into the mystical and galactic realms more than others. But it really doesn't matter where you are on the spectrum of awareness. Millions of us are here on Earth at this time to upshift humanity into a higher level of consciousness. Many of us hold, within our light bodies and DNA, the keys and codes which are now awakening us. We are connecting in powerful ways to Spirit, to the mystical worlds, and to the multi-dimensional aspects of our collective existence. Everyone will open up, remember, and be activated in the sequence and timing that is right for them. Millions of people are now awakening and coming to know the truth that we are all Source energy. We are all aspects of the Divine Light, the Divine Presence, God. Our inner guidance systems are kicking into high gear.

Chapter Four

Why I'm Not Afraid To Die

I've noticed that, generally, our beliefs about death usually go one of two ways: either towards beauty and heaven, or towards fear and hell. Unfortunately, most people lean towards fear, and this is why: our historical and collective programming around death runs deep and has devolved over the last two centuries. Only recently – about the last 50 years – has a growing new awareness about the concepts of death and spirituality emerged. The truth of our spiritual existence is bubbling up in people's awareness and it can't be stopped; our time is now.

In ancient times, when tribes and early cultures lived in tune with Natural Law, they had a deep and sacred connection with the cosmic and spiritual realms. They honoured and celebrated death with great reverence. The cycles of life and death were integrated into the fabric of daily life, and considered very natural. Death was seen a natural bridge into the spiritual afterlife and wasn't feared at all. Cultures even celebrated death with sacred ceremony and rituals. The Egyptians, for example, took great care to prepare the body for its journey to the next world. They built temples, prepared the bodies with great care, and entombed their departed with riches and goods they would need on the other side. In stark contrast, the modern unaware human (instilled with religious and theological rhetoric) now views the inevitable end and passing over as a miserable and scary event. This leaves many to struggle with a concept of dying that is steeped in fear and uncertainty. Do you ever wonder what we become after we lose these human bodies and our earthly identities?

My NDE Showed Me That Our End is Not "The End"

Have you ever wondered how you would feel when faced with your imminent death? What would be on your mind? Honestly, I never gave it a second thought early in my life. Most of us don't think of these things until well into our mature years as 'time is running out' and when the possibility of dying is more likely. However, in that very moment when my car was spinning out on black ice and it was obvious how this was going to end, the subject got very personal in a flash. Now, granted, I was not faced with a slow and prolonged closure to my life in a hospital, with a devastating illness where I would have had time to reflect on the business of dying. My brush with death was a surprise and happened within a few minutes. I was truly amazed by the process. Everything slowed down, time stood still, and I could clearly hear the thoughts going on in my head. I wasn't thinking about how painful this could be. I wasn't thinking that I was too young to die, or of what was waiting for me on the other side. None of these concerns were running through my mind. It was like I was in a soundproof bubble; I didn't even hear the car crashing or anything in my surroundings. Instead, what I experienced was an indescribable sense of peace and surrender. My whole being was aware and completely content knowing that this was my time to leave. A flood of immense peace and acceptance came over me. It surprised me, and I remember thinking, *"Dawn, you're so calm considering..."* I took my hands off the steering wheel and said, *"Here we go."* I don't remember any 'human' thing after that until I was swished back into my body as the car was rolling down the embankment. I am sure I was held in the arms of the angels as they ushered me from my body before impact. This embrace was glorious. What I experienced on the other side for my brief stay was equally glorious. **This is why I'm not afraid to die.** I know death is not the end of our experience. We exist beyond our bodies, formless and Divine.

I am here to tell you, my friends, that what we perceive as the end is not "the end." On the contrary, death is a beautiful and natural doorway to a spiritual reality beyond your greatest expectations and beliefs.

Different cultures fondly refer to dying as a trip over the rainbow bridge, passing beyond the veil, going back home, rebirthing into our spiritual truths, or returning to the light. There are so many beautiful descriptions. Why we lost these beautiful and natural connections to our spiritual life is beyond the scope and intention of this book, but I challenge you to step out of the modern reductionistic and separation paradigm and embrace what you intrinsically know about death, but have forgotten.

These are some of the common existential questions and concerns people often have around dying:
- What will happen when I'm gone?
- What if I get lost on the way to Heaven?
- Is there really a Heaven, and is it reserved for the chosen few?
- What if I cease to exist all together?
- What if I get trapped in the in-between worlds – the bardos – forever?
- What if I go to hell?
- What if dying is painful and scary, maybe terrifying?
- What if I am all alone on my journey beyond and don't know what to do or where to go?

So many fears have been placed in our minds through books, movies, and religious teachings. Our industrial world has removed us from the natural beauty and cycles of life and death. We no longer witness the dying process in our homes and natural settings with our beloveds. We have become removed and buffered from our loved ones as they take the passage into the spiritual worlds of God. The end of life is often handled by the medical gods. The majority of people die in hospitals or institutions where qualified medical staff are the ushers out of this world. They serve as a buffer between us and our loved ones passing over into the worlds beyond. We've lost the understanding, the sacredness, and the holiness of transitioning into the spiritual worlds. We are not fully present in sacred ways to usher our brethren back home over the rainbow bridge. This "death" is the moment we've been waiting for: it's the moment of full remembrance of who we truly are - pure light, pure energy, pure love, pure Spirit, formless and timeless.

If you've ever had the honour of being with a loved one passing into the spiritual worlds, and they are conscious and not caught in programmed fear or resistance, you will notice how peaceful and sometimes incredibly joyous they are. Smiles come to their faces, their eyes brighten, their bodies relax. They are getting glimpses of the other side and the angels are gathering to usher them home. It's truly delightful and a cause for celebration. You can feel and sometimes see the energy infusing the room with pure love and light. It's a thing of beauty.

Formless pure love is exactly what I experienced during my NDE. I found myself part of the eternal and infinite creation of what I could sense was consciousness, or pure energy. Nothing was separate, solid, or had a name; I felt the vast universal consciousness that connects us all. You and I are part of this eternal consciousness, which in that moment seemed to be everywhere and always, infinite and miraculous, full of pure love. God was everywhere and everything. If my words could properly describe what I experienced beyond the veil, you would be truly astounded. In this vast field of source energy, our souls live on, forever. **Our body dies, but we never truly die.**

One might dare to say that death is Divine. Coming to the perfect Divine ending of this dense human physical form and transitioning fully into Spirit is a pinnacle experience. Consider death as an amazing release and homecoming, if you would. If we could change the way we view death or the anticipation of our death, into alignment with what my NDE showed me, we would no longer live or die in fear, right? In fact, when a loved one passed over, we'd want to hold a party to celebrate, not a funeral to mourn. We would hold space with friends and family for the journey home with pure joy and ecstasy. We'd literally midwife a new birth – a spiritual birth – as our loved one stepped into a new creation of consciousness. This would be as death was intended to be.

I know this may not sit well with some, and that's perfectly okay. I don't say this to take away from the loss we feel after a loved one leaves this physical plane. We all need time to adjust and adapt to not having our beloveds physically present in our lives anymore. And we should honour our adjustment process. When I lost my mother, we had tears, then we celebrated with good wine and Italian-style food. The family healing was beautiful and palpable. Ritual, no matter what form it takes, is an important aspect to our lives, and we all need something to honour significant changes.

Anthropologically, ritual was the cornerstone of our ancestors' lives, and we have lost this wisdom along the way. In full disclosure, when my mom passed, it wasn't all fun, food, wine, and stories. We had a traditional funeral and graveside gathering. It was what the church and family expected, but not very personal, intimate, or sacred in my opinion. It felt like a pomp and circumstance display. As they laid her body into the family crypt, I did "lose it" for a while. A sudden raw, primal, and guttural sob exploded out of me. It felt like a knife in my body and I went cold. What I was experiencing at that very moment was the cutting of the energetic cord from my mother to me. It was dramatic and visceral, and I had to process that disconnection in an instant. With so many eyes on me, there was no personal, private, or sacred space to fully feel this moment. Everyone around me thought I was just overcome with grief and sadness, but I knew what was truly going on in my heart and soul. It was very okay and very natural.

The experience of losing a loved one deserves and requires time, patience, and compassion as we adapt to the change. But the depth of our suffering and the stories we tell ourselves about the loss and grief will determine our emotional wellness for days or years afterwards. I am sure you've seen or know of someone who has lost a loved one and has experienced this kind of deep emotional pain and turmoil. Years, perhaps even decades, after their loved one's passing, they are still stricken with grief and have not recovered from the loss in any healthy way. My beloved friends, if you've been gifted with a glimpse of the "other side" like I have, I promise that you would not get stuck in the muck and grief. You would not sit in the dark pain for long, or even at all. You would instead shed your tears, process the loss, and smile in your heart through it all, knowing your loved ones are continuing their journey in all the worlds of God. You would be happy for their journey back home to their natural and expanded state of pure love and light. You would feel nothing but joy for your loved one! You would welcome it without judgment and with full love and acceptance. I am aware that what I just said is, for some, a big pill to swallow, but it is the truth as I have seen and experienced it. Anyone reading this who has suffered with loss and might be feeling uncomfortable, please know in your heart that no one is passing judgment here. Your experience is not to be judged by others or even by you. This is a life experience that demands compassion and understanding. No one is ever at fault here. We know what we know at the time; we feel what we feel at the time; we experience our reality according to our awareness at the time. It's all Divine. Let's instead ask ourselves, "Can I can change grief into acceptance and peace?" Allow me to share more. Let's journey together.

This is what I've come to know about death

- we can't die "wrong"
- a soul exits this life only when it is complete and only then
- if a soul has more evolution to complete or choses to rewrite their contract, their human journey can continue
- there are no accidents or unfortunate events; everything in life is perfectly orchestrated *for* you
- death is never an accident; it's a gift of our soul's completion
- you are not your body – you have a body, but you are not your body
- we are all spirits of pure love, light, and frequency/energy
- we are a living embodied consciousness in human form; our souls are formless in spirit
- we are expanded awareness, connected to everything, and part of the greater universe, a living entity of consciousness
- we are both energy and form; this is the duality of our existence
- we don't end when we die; we continue to live on in all the spiritual worlds of God
- your soul gets to choose what you want to experience in this life
- the beautiful union with God/Source is almost unexplainable in human words
- everything we thought was solid and physical is an illusion
- everything is made of light, which is frequency and energy
- even pain and suffering is light, just under pressure, and holds

- density when in human form
- when we unconditionally and radically love our pain and release emotional core wounding, we can heal
- reuniting with the unified field, which many call God, is "Going Home"
- home is completion, a blissful reunion with the Divine core of our being
- the idea of "hell" is just separation from God
- we are not separate from anything; our separateness is an illusion
- we are eternal consciousness living in a human body for a short time
- we are unconditionally loved by God/Source; we *are* that love
- God exists in us, flows through us, and is all around us
- we are sparks of the Divine

When we eventually come to know the truth of who and what we are during this human journey, then we can step out of all the fear, and all the worry. We can step out of the programming and influences the world is bombarding us with, and be born into a life that knows only love. If we understand and identify ourselves as an aspect of the Divine, a spark of God, of Creation, knowing we are *not* separate from God, then it's easier to understand that there is a Divine plan playing out. And it's your plan, a plan that your soul created before your birth, your human incarnation. Everything in your life is unfolding splendidly and perfectly, and nothing happens to you that, at a higher level of understanding, you do not want to have happen to you. Imagine if you walked around with this understanding. I bet you would never get bent out of shape again over life's happenings. I suspect fear would fade out of your life and in its place would be acceptance, love, and joy.

> *"And it is in dying that we are born to eternal life."*
> **Prayer of St. Francis of Assisi**

Do you remember in the Prayer of St. Francis where it says this? This line in the prayer sums it up. Really take a moment to soak in these words; they are the truth and this concept has been hidden in plain sight.

I personally sang and said this prayer a million times in church and I overlooked its true meaning.

In this era of human transformation and awakening, it's time to dissolve the archaic hell and brimstone beliefs around death. They have kept us in fear far too long, and they are an illusion. We never die. We have always existed in the worlds of God and we will continue to soar in the worlds of God forever. The God presence I experienced and the Heaven I saw was the furthest thing from Hell you can imagine – quite the opposite in every way. Remember, my friends, you are an individuated aspect of the Divine. I invite humanity to embrace and celebrate our collective transition time and to let go of fear and overwhelm. Release the need to be stricken with loss and grief. We can shed tears of joy as we honour the rebirth of a soul into full consciousness with the unified field of love. We can open our hearts to a life free of the idea of separateness from others and God. We are part of the vast tapestry of life, and we are all important, and needed, and in service to each other in ways we can't even imagine. This is what I experienced on the other side; it's what I can share with you from my personal experience. I cannot put into human words the *feeling* and *knowing* of this. I guess you'll have to take my word for it. Or not; it is your choice.

What Else Prompted Me to Write This Book?

Besides wanting to share my NDE and elucidate the truth of our spiritual existence, the other driving force behind writing this book came from my experiences as a health care practitioner. I have keenly observed, witnessed, and held space for many patients over the last 30 years. They have shared their most intimate and vulnerable fears and worries about illness and death with me. I can't even begin to tell you about the intense worry and fear that people are operating with day after day. Their burdens are heavy as they struggle to navigate their lives in a world where it's polite to put on a happy face and pretend like everything is okay, or post on social media the amazing aspects of their lives, all the while suffering in silence.

Fear and worry grip them so tightly that they can't find the joy in life. It is very sad to witness because often the suffering comes from learned programming. People live with immense anguish, loneliness, and despair. I wish I could wave a magic wand and take it all away to ease their suffering, but I can't. I am not their rescuer, but I am a lightworker, and a portal – a loving support for those who are ready to heal their wounds. I wrote this book **to help ease pain and suffering in any way I can, through sharing my experience, knowledge, and gifts. The intention of this book is to open the hearts of beloved souls to a remembrance of their true essence and to impart a deep knowing that illness and death are not a failure at all. We are Spirits of pure love. We came from love and we will return to love; there is nothing to fear in death.**

Everything we are choosing to experience in life – all the illness and pain – is specifically crafted by our souls for our own evolution. Humanity has a distorted view of difficulties: whatever goes "wrong" is a problem. I'm here to tell you that what we experience is never a problem. My "Life Line Technique" teacher, Darren Weissman, teaches that *"nothing is a problem, just a portal to the next best version of ourselves."* Everything, no matter how terrible or challenging, is an opportunity to buff off the spiky edges of our ego and polish our soul.

As a modern mystic and Naturopathic Doctor, I take the time to get to know my patients and their stories. My clients are never just a cluster of symptoms; they are a universe unto themselves waiting to be seen, heard, discovered, and held in love. I am keenly aware that our bodies speak to the psychological underpinnings of trauma and wounding, even from past generations. Put another way, *disease is the biological solution to our unresolved conflict or trauma.* Our bodies literally hold the score. Every emotion that remains unresolved retains an energetic pattern in the body, and in the informational field around the body. Each emotion has a specific frequency that reflects the unresolved psychological issue. This can build up resistance in the field, blocking energy flow and informing the body in deleterious ways. Eventually, this gets expressed as physical illness in the body. Before we get really sick, our body-mind forms habitual patterns of energy and produces symptoms in an effort to get our attention. I explain it to my patients like this: *"Your body is trying to have a conversation with you. It's not purposefully crapping out on you. It's trying to get your attention to see what needs healing. It is raising up the white flag and waving it around, waiting for you to notice. I would be happy to help you decipher and identify what's really going on if you are willing."* This approach demands self-responsibility, self-compassion, self-inquiry, and resolve. Worth it in my opinion, though.

Our bodies are not meant to hold onto trauma and conflicts. If we keep loading on the anger, resentment, fear and worry, it's no wonder we start to feel unwell. Let me explain it like this. Everything in our world is frequency: the sun, a table, a flower, a mineral, water, food, a thought, a word, a belief, a remedy…everything. Depending on how we choose to live, we can steep ourselves in low vibrational frequency at every turn, especially if we are stuck in buildings all day and not getting out into nature. Or, on the other hand, we can bathe ourselves in positive higher vibrational activities and environments. Put another way, frequencies can either heal or harm us. I invite you to simply get curious. Are you adding healing frequencies into your life, or pounding yourself with negative harmful ones? For instance, are you holding onto all that unprocessed frustration, stuffing your emotions, and eating "non-food"? Or are you taking a sacred pause, releasing and processing the frustration, and allowing the healing frequency of Mother Earth or Source to rebalance you? This is just one example; I think you get the idea.

I invite you to begin the process of listening to your body's conversation. Get curious and figure out your unique process of healing. Include large doses of love and compassion for yourself along the way. Perhaps you haven't thought of yourself or your body as sacred. It's made of Divine light, designed with self-regulating intelligence and an incredible capacity to heal. I have seen intense beautiful light emanate from high vibrational people while in healing sessions with them. It's wondrous and miraculous to witness.

Ancient Chinese doctors were cognizant of this light energy. They called it Qi and discovered that it flowed in channels and pathways called meridians. They knew about natural law, and the importance of living in balance with it. They also knew that in order for the body to stay healthy and heal, energy needed to flow openly. They understood the five element cycles, and used simple Qigong and Tai Chi exercises, or acupuncture and herbal medicine, as powerful tools for healing. They also understood the impact that emotions have on every organ of the body. For instance, if you find yourself with kidney stones or kidney disease, it is wise to ask yourself: "What fear am I holding onto?" The energy of fear harms the kidneys. Likewise, the energy of grief harms the lungs, etc. There are some practices in the Appendix section of the book to get you started and help you process emotions to keep your organs healthy.

Another fascinating thing about our bodies is that our DNA holds an intelligent original imprint that, if left undisturbed and not tampered with, will keep our bodies healthy forever. But, living in a world of ever-increasing levels of toxins and stressors makes it harder to stay in our highest state of functionality. We have polluted our world and our bodies with too much junk. And since we also hold onto our trauma and woundings, piling on more debris, is it any wonder that we are so often sick? Day after day, our bodies do their best to compensate until they can no longer adapt. Then they fall into physical decompensation and dysregulation, resulting in disease. Supporting our bodies from all the harmful toxins is beyond the scope of this book. I encourage you to investigate Natural medicine and healing modalities to assist you in staying free of disease.

Meanwhile, beginning a journey of self-inquiry to understand your personal stressors, woundings, and programs can open the door to fully healing from them. Not everyone wants to go that deep, and I understand that. I encourage you to find a therapist or healer who can hold space to hear you, see you, and support you on your journey. I envision medicine of the future as an integration of mind, body, and spirit. I hope for the return of sacred ceremony and the honouring of our spiritual existence. I believe the true definition of healing (real healing, not just managing symptoms) is this: coming back to wholeness, and circling back to the truth that you are an individuated aspect of the Divine. Individuated, but never separated from God. We have sacred bodies that house our beautiful souls. It is our job and our privilege to take care of these vehicles, but there is more to us than flesh and bones. Wouldn't you agree?

What about Worry and Fear?

If, magically, I could have the full essence of this book land in your heart, we could instantly start shifting the collective experience over these human emotions called fear and worry! I know it's not just up to me, and we are all here to discover our truths in unique and perfect ways. But wow, if I had a dime for every time someone said, *"I'm worried about..."*, I would be rich. Worry is one of the biggest programs of all and guess what? It is rooted in FEAR. Have you ever heard the acronym for fear?

False

Evidence

Appearing

Real

Remember this acronym the next time you find yourself worrying about something, my friend.

I invite you to stay on this journey with me as we unpack fear and worry. If worry is just an energetic extension of fear, and fear is an illusion made up in our minds, why are we in the business of worrying? No judgment here. Hold yourself in compassion as you read further. At a primitive level, a healthy level of fear is understandable; we are wired to survive. However, the level of fear and worry in this society is boiling over. We have all experienced worry or fear about something at some point of our lives, myself included. But the habit of worrying all the time creates perpetual fear and stress, causing a leak of our life-force essence. As a result, you have less vital life-force energy to heal and regulate your body. This is a recipe for illness. Visiting Chinese medicine again, we know that worry causes a weakness of your stomach/spleen energy. This depletion can cause maldigestion, varicose veins, prolapses, bleeding ulcers, heavy bleeding, swollen spleen, etc. I see this frequently, especially with female patients. Often, they are aware of their worry habits and want to stop, but they learned it from their mother, and she from her mother, and up the family tree it goes. It is difficult to change such ingrained patterns of behavior unless you are determined and motivated to do so. Sometimes, our social structure justifies the habit of worrying because it is seen as an act of caring for someone or something. But if we give the program of worry an open lane in our lives, it can run the show. The groove on the record grows deeper and deeper as we play the same old program, over and over.

"Worry is like a rocking chair ... it keeps you busy but it doesn't get you anywhere!"

Marcel Bellehumeur

The more mature I get, combined with the wisdom gained from my NDE experience, the more I see worry as an exaggerated illusion. I ask you, when has worrying about a situation ever really helped? Holding onto worry, even though well-intentioned, will take your health down, physically and mentally. I regularly share these concepts about worry with clients. I lovingly point out that worry is not ever going to change the situation. Instead, worry amplifies your own frequency of worry and attracts more of it (that's called Law of Attraction) and makes you sick. Remember, the energy of worry is a very low vibration. When you worry, you not only weaken yourself but, unintentionally, the person you're worrying about as well.

If it seems like such a useless emotion, why the heck do we have such a thing as worry anyway? Well, worry can have a positive spin, believe it or not. Worry can serve as a portal – an opportunity to change and evolve, and become that next best version of yourself. It can catalyze you to embody a higher frequency and awareness, and provide a springboard to a new level of emotional wellness. If we all committed to transforming our worry into peace and contentment, the whole world would be a better place. So, the next time you catch yourself worrying, I invite you to raise the vibration and send the energy of love and light to the person or situation instead. Everything heals in love and light.

In closing this chapter, I will share with you something powerful and positive a friend said to me one day during the early days of the Covid Pandemic (or Plandemic, depending on your view). At a time of intense fear, worry, and uncertainty, when most people were operating on external information to guide their actions and make decisions, he put it simply: *"I'm living in faith not fear, Baby."* I'll never forget his exuberance and light at that moment. That's the attitude I wish I could bottle and serve to every human on this planet. So let yourself be curious. Step out of fear-based programming and go to your heart. Tap into your higher Soul Self. When facing your imminent death, what beliefs will you be holding in your heart?

CHAPTER FIVE

Treasure in Your Trauma

"I am here to remind you, my friends, that everything in your life – everything – is in Divine order, even when it feels absolutely terrible."

Dawn Cormier

This bold and challenging statement may trigger some people. It may bring up thoughts like: *"Sure, easy for you to say"*, or *"No way, all this positive thinking stuff is bogus"*, or *"Whatever you tell yourself to sleep well at night."* I understand the subconscious push back.

To be fair, I get why some might wonder how difficult things – even tragic, for that matter – could be for someone's highest good. Perhaps these things are here for a specific purpose. Perhaps these things are actually catalysts for change. Take, for example, the need to step out of an abusive or toxic relationship. Perhaps it's time to let go, or shut it down to allow something new and better to come into our lives. Perhaps our Higher Self is crafting a better outcome for us in the end – something our human self couldn't imagine. Yet, there is more to it than that, so let's dive a little deeper.

Human Trauma & The Meaning of Suffering

Let's back up for a moment. Humans generally don't enjoy suffering. We are, for the most part, programmed to process a "bad" event as something that went terribly wrong. That it was somehow unfair, or a mistake. We tend to believe that suffering is a terrible thing to endure. Fair enough. Our human minds also tend to rationalize and defend our actions and choices to avoid cognitive dissonance. We are really good at this. We argue things like: *"Why should I have to go through this? Why would God make these things happen? I chose to have a life full of joy and happiness; I didn't choose suffering. I'm a good person. My life should be above the suffering that I see all around me",* and so on. We predominantly think this way for two reasons.

The first reason would be our cultural and religious understanding that views suffering as **"a product of the fall, a consequence of human sin against God"** *(Romans 5:12; 1 Corinthians 15:21).* This message, rooted in Biblical times, goes deep into our generational trauma. We have been programmed or influenced to believe that we deserve suffering and struggle because of original sin (our human imperfections, weakness, and worthlessness). With these generational memories and programs running the show, it's easy to understand why we might fall into despair when we have an illness, chronic pain or suffer abuse. The dictionary definition of despair is **"having suffering without meaning."** Now here is the juicy part: Could how we hold the situation or event determine if we suffer or grow from an experience? Spoiler alert: the answer is yes. So, you could say that human suffering is all in the mind, correct? Yes. Human beings have an incredible imagination when it comes to making up an experience of suffering. Coupled with a good memory, it's no wonder we suffer.

In the Journal of Psychology and Psychiatry (2015 edition), a psychiatrist's article concludes this: *"Since suffering is an inevitable part of life, one must try to find meaning in it. Terminally or chronically ill persons despair of their suffering when they do not see any meaning to it. They see it as a waste of life, a useless experience. Hence, they conclude that suffering is meaningless."* Psychiatrist Viktor Frankl writes in this same article, *"Despair is suffering without meaning. Those who despair of their suffering find life unbearable."* Frankl goes on to say, *"Life can be made meaningful ... through the stand we take toward a fate we no longer can change (an incurable disease, an inoperable cancer, or the like). Since human beings have free will, they must choose to see a meaning to their suffering. What makes the difference between despair and meaning?"* Frankl answers: *"The attitude we choose toward suffering."* Speaking as both a medical doctor and a psychiatrist, Frankl says, *"Meaning rests on the attitude the patient chooses toward suffering."* Bingo. The key that unlocks the shackles of trauma or grief is **the attitude we choose.**

Along my journey of life, I have explored many religious and spiritual teachings. I became a Baha'i and I loved the practice. It served me very well for 15 years. The Holy writings gave me understanding and grounded me in many ways. The following writing applied to my physical struggles and gave me guidance and precious hope: **"When calamity striketh, be ye patient and composed. However afflictive your sufferings may be, stay ye undisturbed, and with perfect confidence..."** (selections from the writings of Abdu'l-Baha). The Guardian of the Bahá'í Faith wrote: *"As long as there will be life on earth, there will be also suffering, in various forms and degrees. But suffering, although an inescapable reality, can nevertheless be utilized as a means for the attainment of happiness. This is the interpretation given to it by all the prophets and saints who, in the midst of severe tests and trials, felt happy and joyous and experienced what is best and holiest in life. Suffering is both a reminder and a guide. It stimulates us better to adapt ourselves to our environmental conditions, and thus leads the way to self-improvement.* ***In every suffering one can find a meaning and a wisdom. But it is not always easy to find the secret of that wisdom. It is sometimes only when all our suffering has passed that we become aware of its usefulness.*** *What man considers to be evil turns often to be a cause of infinite blessings."* (Unfolding Destiny, Shoghi

Effendi, p. 434).

Take a deep healing breath here, my friend. Let this sink in. Does your heart feel contented and more supported now? Don't you feel unburdened by those words?

These insights are the features of the incredible universe we live in. Fast forward to our modern age where modern-day seer and scientist Elizabeth Wood says, *"Suffering is good, it is needed. Humans under pressure is evolution."* I agree wholeheartedly with her observation. This perspective gives a spin on suffering that, rather than promoting despair, instead inspires growth, joy, and contentment under all conditions of life. So, the next time you are faced with an enduring situation, a diagnosis, or a calamity, stop and breathe, and recall what you've just read. Become aware and centered, place your hand on your heart, feel the love that you are, and dive into self-inquiry. Take the ride and all the blessings along the way. Everything in your life has meaning and purpose.

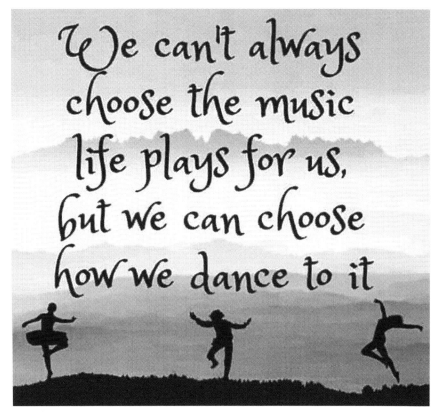

The second reason why humans quickly jump into the pool of suffering is that our primitive brain remembers struggle and suffering from our ancestral past. This trauma is encoded into our DNA. These memories have an important job. They keep us safe and out of suffering; by remembering and learning from the past we can hopefully avoid more trauma in the future. These ancestral memories served us well when we lived in tribes and were vulnerable to the elements and the wild. We had to be vigilant in those times, and hyper-aware of the slightest details of our surroundings so we could sprint into action. That is no longer the case. Most of us don't live in a jungle that poses real physical threats to us on a daily basis. We generally live "safe" lives. However, our minds perceive threats from "frivolous" things, real or imagined, or unproductive programmed ways of thinking. This keeps us in a perpetual stage of fight or flight, and an ongoing state of trauma. This is the definition of modern-day suffering.

As described above, our collective meaning of suffering has had a bad reputation, for far too long. Now having said that, I do not wish more suffering on anyone. It's not always easy or pleasant to navigate. However, in the greater context, as a species we are starting to awaken to new understandings. Psychologists, Messengers of God, Saints, New-thought leaders, Spiritualists and the like have brought forward their sage advice about suffering. I think it's time we take these teachings to heart. It's time to leave the old structures of suffering, fear, and worry, and open our consciousness.

I believe we are beginning to perceive that we are Spirit in a human body; we have a duality of being both energetic and physical beings. Here is more knowledge about the body we live in. Many mystics, scientists, and channels are confirming that our bodies are holding more light frequency than ever before. The photonic energy from the sun is actually changing us. This is a process of evolution in which we transition from Homo sapiens to Homo luminous, holding less density and more light. We are literally changing at a cellular, DNA level. We are evolving in the cycle of the cosmos. In fact, science has proven that every thought we have influences and informs our DNA. That's great news. It puts us in the driver's seat. Not only can our thoughts and feelings change the meaning of our suffering, they can also support healing at the level of our DNA.

As we witness the structures around us crumbling (physical, social, economic, political, medical, industrial, climatic), we are free to move out of fear, judgment, control, manipulation, top-down power structures, separation, and segregation. This is our time for change, and as you know, change isn't always so comfortable. But we don't have to suffer during calamity or unsettling times. Like a piece of coal under pressure, eventually we will emerge as a diamond. This is a time in humanity of punctuated equilibrium; it's an opportunity for positive change and evolution.

I don't profess to be an expert in this area. There are more advanced and awakened human souls than me who understand these aspects much better. What I can offer you is what I've come to know since my NDE and how it confirms this narrative. **We are light, we are energy, we are formless, we are connected in oneness, we exist in a field of source energy, we are pure love – and it is our birth right to know this**. We are more powerful than we've ever been taught in our schools and churches and by our media and governments. We are of God Source – a spark of the Divine. These existing structures have kept us in the frequency of fear and control far too long. They are being dismantled. We cannot move forward in the evolution and expansion of our species if the old paradigm is still in power. So, make way for the new, my friends.

The moment we realize that Death is not final, scary, or a failure, we are free. This deep truthful knowing is not solely reserved for the moment of death or after an NDE. Life is full of overflowing moments to cultivate our souls, and endless opportunities abound to discover these realizations. The beauty, grace, and gift of this precious human life is that we may choose to use any one event or situation as a platform for gaining higher awareness and insights. **You don't have to die to have a soulful remembrance.** It's within your awareness now if you tap into your heart.

Life continues to serve up opportunities in the guise of various people, places, situations, events, and traumas all curated to assist us in our soul's evolution. Everything occurs in our lives to help us clarify and focus our connections and awareness of this Divine soul experience we are having. If we choose to see these events as serving to bring us back to our inner sanctuary, therein lies the gift.

Sometimes we can become disappointed in our bodies, or frustrated with our physical limitations and illness. But when we shift to being grateful for the way our body is trying to get our attention so that we see what needs to be healed, we step into a mind-set of finding **treasure in our trauma**. While these treasures might be "gifts in strange wrapping paper," embrace them, my friend. As Wayne Dyer so eloquently said, *"When we fundamentally change how we see things, the things we see change."* Our whole life takes on a new level of freedom. Embrace the gifts from your Soul. Be open to seeing everything with grace and gratitude. That is the definition of freedom, isn't it?

A Hero's Example

We have established that there is meaning in our suffering. Perhaps you've seen it in action in your own life. For example, someone you know who was diagnosed with a serious bone cancer and the only option the doctors gave them was to amputate the limb. Our first reaction might likely be, *"That's terrible"* or, *"It's so sad they had to lose their leg to cancer."* This common reaction is ingrained into our programming. Now let's take a look at this well-known example of what appeared to be a tragedy, but wasn't. Terry Fox had his leg amputated to stop the spread of a serious bone cancer that threatened the rest of his body. In the face of his bleak situation, Terry could have chosen to feel sorry for himself, or resented his body for getting sick. He could have been angry about his circumstances, or hated the doctors who tried to save his life, or any other possible victim responses and reactions to a situation like this. That wasn't the case. Terry had the insight and awareness to understand that losing a limb didn't make him any less of a person. It did not detract from his life's meaning or purpose. On the contrary, he found *"meaning in his suffering"* and *"treasure in his trauma."* He chose to use his situation to bring national awareness to cancer therapy and treatments. By running across the country, raising money, finding sponsors, and documenting his whole journey through the media, he brought tears to the eyes of Canadians with his story of resilience and courage. He took what many would think of as a horrible situation and turned it into a blessing. It was through his cancer journey that he would change the world for the better. He is the example of turning lemons into lemonade.

I don't bring up this example to trigger any shame or "less than" emotions for anyone. I lovingly bring this to light to exemplify that we are the creators of our own reality. We all have multiple opportunities – maybe not as grand as Terry's, but nonetheless, meaningful situations that provide evolution and awareness for ourselves, and for those who witness our journeys. Our reality will become what we *choose*, regardless of the outcome, and our growth will depend on how we see it, how we hold it, how we perceive it. This will determine the beauty or tragedy we will ultimately feel.

Where Do We Go from Here?

"It is a matter of what you choose to look at."
Neale Donald Walsch

So, what do you do with all your suffering and symptoms? I recommend you have the courage to unpack all of it and begin looking into the meaning. Suspend judgment and become curious. Ask questions like: *What are you here to tell me? What are you here to show me? What needs to be seen? What needs to heal? What needs to change?*

Truth is, until we get to the meaning of why we are having a certain experience, we can't fully heal. Our physical pain is here to tell us something; our emotional pain is here to speak to us, too. This is exactly what happened to me after my crash. I have no shame in admitting that for years, I was trapped in disabling pain and suffering. I wanted to function – as a mother, as a wife, as a doctor – but it took so much effort to keep on going that I became exhausted. As I described earlier in Chapter 2, I desperately sought relief and a cure. I looked for a physical answer to my physical pain. Although it was wonderful to have that relief, it was a fleeting, short-term solution only. Once I got stressed or run down again, bam! My neck would get unstable, leading to days of muscle spasms and pain. It was quite the dance. I was tired of it, and I'm sure everyone in my family was tired of it, too. I felt like some external puppeteer was pulling strings in my life. I feared that at any moment, I would be unable to move.

The road to healing and wholeness was a long one for me. This was exactly how I needed to experience it, in Divine and perfect ways. However, the treasure in my trauma was two-fold. The first gift was coming home to my authentic self – a humbling road to spiritual mastery which continues to this day. And I'm not shy to say I've come a long way, baby. The second gift was the chance to learn a myriad of healing therapies and techniques that I otherwise wouldn't have become familiar with. Now I use them to ease others' discomfort and help them on their road to healing. If I didn't *"have to"* do the work on myself, I never would have been able to serve others with them. Physical therapies are a welcome relief and often warranted to make our lives more manageable. However, unrelenting and recurring illness or pain patterns often need more than a physical approach. To be fully resolved, they also need spiritual and emotional healing. Physical symptoms scream at us to look deeper at underlying issues and root causes, which are held in the body and expressed through it. Once we unravel their unique meaning, we release the pain or illness. Then we are truly healed, becoming whole once again in mind, body, and spirit – the perfect trifecta of our human experience.

In my healing journey, I found myself magnetically drawn toward different modalities for healing, based on various spiritual, emotional, and energetic processing techniques. It was like a door opened and a flashing light pointed right at them, saying, *"Go here."* I trusted this guidance completely because it felt so right for me. My higher Soul Self lead me to my healing within these mystical and energetic realms. I learned so much on this amazing adventure. I soon realized that my repeating patterns of pain needed time, compassionate inquiry, loving awareness, and heart-felt gratitude. Little by little, the layers were revealed and healed, and I learned to listen with compassion and love. I learned to trust in the dictates of my soul. It all culminated in a final healing ceremony, and I have no doubt in my heart that this was crafted by design. Your design will probably be different and unfold in your own unique way. Be patient and keep your heart open. You'll get there.

Nowadays, when I have a hiccup in the road and notice a symptom or emotional experience that needs processing, I grab for an energy-psychology modality from my tool box: meditation, EFT, the Emotion Code, Body Code, Toplakan directives, Reiki, or one of my Quantum Healing techniques. Any of these will get me back on track. Sometimes I visit an energy healer or a holistic practitioner. It's important to take care of this sacred body. On your healing journey, it's important not to let the judgments of others get in your way. Your road to healing is sacred. Honour your journey in life. Don't let the illness, or the eventuality of death scare you. Remember: you are not this body; you only inhabit it. You, my friend, are a Spirit of pure love and light. Your body is mortal, but your soul is not!

As you approach the imminent moment of your death, I can guarantee you, you will realize how little of your 3D life mattered. As you leave your body and depart from your physical density, you will realize that your "struggle" was for nothing, just like Daniel Blasutti did. As he teetered on the edge of his mortality, he realized his ladder of success was leaning up against the wrong building all along. He had "wasted" so much of his time striving for what really didn't have meaning. Now, he didn't judge himself and beat himself up about this. On the contrary, he wanted to shout to the world that the 3D importance we give life isn't real. He wanted people to stop walking through life disconnected from spiritual truth. Humanity still has some evolving to go through, but I'm sure Daniel would be excited to see so many souls waking up to their own spiritual truths. We are all on our road to mastery, so don't judge yourself or others. Rather, offer more love and compassion as we all continue to take steps of beauty.

As a reminder of staying true to my path, I tattooed the artwork depicted below on my arm as I launched this book writing venture. It is a symbol of my continued journey and purpose, reminding me of my inner spiritual compass. It is there to remind me that I am never alone; Crow Spirit is always with me.

What is your symbol?

CHAPTER SIX

The Path Forward

"Whatever your path, it is Perfect and Divinely crafted for you."
Dawn Cormier

Everyone's spiritual path is highly personal and as life unfolds (*for you, not to you*) you may find yourself investigating many aspects and avenues of spiritual growth. You will naturally follow your soul-inspired interests and follow the trail of breadcrumbs as they are perfectly laid out for you. Be ready for the synchronicities that will burst forth as you grow and evolve. Regardless of what paths you take, or which you stick to, you will find the ones that speak to you, and are perfect for you at the time. Embrace all the experiences life offers you. Even if they feel really crappy, each and every one of them are gifts, divinely offered for your soul's evolution. Have you ever thought of all the little choices we make in life? They are like nano-opportunities. Life isn't about one big decision; it's all the little choices that add up. These nano-choices can have many different trajectories, all of them having their own service to your soul in the long run. Rather than getting frustrated with yourself for "making the wrong choice" or "taking the wrong route" begin the practice of self-inquiry and compassion. Since the eventual outcome or event is here to serve you, let's begin to listen and unpack it. For instance, without judgment, begin to ask yourself questions like these: *"Why has this happened? Why is this coming up for me? What needs to be seen here? What is coming up to be healed deep inside of me? What is the pattern that requires transmuting?"* Once you get the hang of it, and get into the habit of self-inquiry, it's quite easy.

Perhaps this example will assist you to start the process for yourself. I had an ongoing pattern that was showing itself in my clinical practice for a while that was super frustrating for me. I had a run of clients who were canceling their appointments, without respectful advanced notice, for what I perceived as trivial reasons. It wasn't the cancellations themselves that frustrated me. It was the darn inconvenience, both for me, my staff, and other clients. I had a long waiting list of very sick people, desperate to get into the schedule. They could have used that precious appointment time. But it wasn't possible to rebook on such short notice, and clients were missing out. This was getting exhausting and I was getting triggered left, right and centre. I felt taken advantage of and personally disrespected, and I felt badly for those clients losing out. About 50% of the time, when these last-minute cancellations happened, it turns out it was the universe shifting the playing field and opening up a fantastic door for someone else. In these cases, things were divinely timed for everyone. However, this old frustrating pattern kept creeping into my experience and it was messing with me. One day, I finally decided to sit with it instead of getting frustrated. I sat in meditation and asked, *"What is this here to teach me? What needs to be healed for me to move on?"* The answer dropped right in. The frequency of 'injustice' had come up to be transmuted from generations and generations of experiences. It ran very deep. I realized the people who were cancelling were just playing their part in my life to get my attention so I could process and heal this energetic pattern. I opened ceremony, invited in my lineage, did some heart commands and directives, and processed the age-old pattern of injustice. It felt so good to get free of that energetic pattern and move on – like a weight had been lifted off my shoulders. I could have continued my frustration around what felt like disrespect and injustice, but sitting in self-love and inquiry was the ticket. This example speaks to the saying that it's not the destination in life or the outcomes that determine our success or mastery; it's how we choose to hold the situation or opportunity that counts.

Entering into and embracing your own spiritual path is a very private journey. It is solely for your own personal soul evolution, which will be in alignment with your soul contract for this life stream. Even though at some point you may stray away from how you were raised or taught, don't worry. You will always find your own path and way of understanding, and applying spirituality in your life. Your job is to simply to honour your own growth and calling. This is your soul signature calling out to you, despite what your friends or family may think of your ventures. I can promise that if you don't follow your path, you either will be downright miserable, or Spirit (Soul Self) will tap you on your shoulder in creative or sometimes dramatic ways to get your attention. You may hear, remember, or recognize something or someone that comes into your life and causes you to take notice. You may be aware that it's the calling of your soul – maybe not right away, but if you keep your heart open, the alignment will happen.

How Do I Know What Is My Path?

First of all, don't fret or worry, my friend. You are already on your Divine Path and it will continue to unfold for you in perfectly Divine ways, guaranteed. It's not that you will miss something, or do the wrong thing, or pick the wrong thing. Remember what we have covered so far in this book. Maybe you're thinking, "I don't know what's next for me" or, "How can I be sure?" These questions are natural. Even if you've come into this life stream fully awake and evolved, activated and ready to go, refining your compass can take some work. I sometimes still have difficulty listening to my own frequency amidst all the noise around me. It took years of self-discovery and experience to learn how to go inward to follow my truth. The practice of tuning into your soul for intuitive guidance will bring you joy, wisdom, and peace, and will expand your capacity for love. You will begin to finally feel at home, in alignment, and in harmony with your whole being. You will no longer be afraid of illness, death, or challenges. You will be able to discern false information or energy that isn't in alignment with yourself. You will experience your authentic self and freedom from things that distract you from your true human nature. In the words of Reverend Michael Bernard Beckwith, "Only that which is found from within can bring you joy and contentment. The external is powerless to satisfy the inner spirit." I encourage you to focus your attention on that which is real, not the external, and you will undergo a permanent change in consciousness. I promise. So, let's spend some time talking a little about our **internal guidance system**.

Tuning into Your Soul's Inner Guidance

We are all intuitive and psychic. It's part of who we are, and we are Divinely designed as such. Despite what you have been taught to believe about yourself, you are your best guide and advisor. You have everything you already need. Society has successfully programmed us into believing we have to go outside ourselves for direction and answers. We have also been taught that we have only five senses (taste, touch, seeing, hearing, smelling). However, we have another sense – the gift of psychic awareness. This is your 6th sense, connected to the third eye. The third eye is also known as your pineal gland. It is the only gland in your body that is crystalline in structure, and can perceive energy and photons of light. Your pineal gland can pick up what your physical eyes cannot. When fully opened and developed, this is what allows psychics to "see" beyond the veil. Don't get caught in the trap of comparison if you were not gifted with this kind of psychic awareness. It will open up in perfect timing for you. I know you may want to have it all now; I did too when I started my spiritual awakening. But you will be surprised – maybe even delighted – with how amazing your sixth sense is already.

Before you jump on board with wanting to "open up" your third eye, I would like to draw your attention to something I feel is more important: your Heart Mind and Gut-mind.

The Three Minds and The Three Energy Centres

Let's have fun with this concept of the three minds for inner guidance. It is said that the longest journey in one's life is only 12 inches long: the distance from your head to your heart. That's right on the money. The heart centre is where we feel, and we live in a feeling universe. It's no coincidence that your heart centre also emits the largest electromagnetic field of your whole body, for very good reason.

Science has discovered we have three "brain-centres" in the body:
- Brain-mind
- Heart-mind
- Gut-mind

As we go about our day-to-day life thinking predominantly with our brain-mind to function much of the time, we have come to believe that the brain-mind has higher intelligence. It's our air traffic control centre, as it were, and we rely on it heavily. But it's not the sharpest tool in our tool box. Scientific research has found that everything starts in the heart centre. For example, when we "see" something that prompts an emotional response, you would logically think that we take in the information through our optic nerve, which then signals the brain, we process it, and then have a response. Surprisingly, that's not how it works. It's been proven that the first system to respond to external stimuli is the heart field. Science has detected fluctuations in the heart field first, and then the rest of the body responds. The experiments of Dr. Bruce Lipton, Dr. Joe Dispenza, and the Heart Math Institute have proved these findings over and over. We now know that the heart contains about 50,000 sensory neurites, and surprisingly, it actually functions like a mini-brain. When we "feel" something with our heart-mind, the frequency of our feeling then sends a signal to the higher centers of the brain-mind and we get a response. If we were to operate fully from our brain-mind center, we would be playing out a subconscious program a whopping 95% of the time. Only 5% of the time we can conjure up a new thought pattern based on new information, consciously responding instead of reacting subconsciously.

We also have another guidance system called the gut-mind. Firstly, the gut houses trillions of individual conscious living bacteria, which have their own intelligence and cellular communication network amongst the diverse species living there. So essentially, we have a whole community of living entities, with their own consciousness, living in our gut. Secondly, the gut houses a system of interconnected enteric neurons and they also function like a mini-brain. Thirdly, the gut area encompasses an energy centre called the Lower Dantian, also called the Hara. Different from a chakra, it's a very powerful area believed to be the seat of life force energy in the body, and related to higher states of consciousness. This lower Dantian holds primary importance as it nourishes the higher two Dantians – the heart (middle Dantian, representing the seat of Qi) and the Third Eye (upper Dantian, representing spirit and intuition). This is a Chinese system of energy that directly correlates with the three minds we have just described. Interestingly, the Chinese don't give preference or importance to one centre over the other, as they work as an interactive intelligent system. However, the energy flows from the lower centre (the gut) to the middle centre (the heart), then to the upper centre (the mind), not the other way around. This suggests that the brain-mind is actually of lowest importance on the totem pole, which is indeed the case. I'm sure everyone can relate to the unsettled feeling in your tummy when you are upset or have to do something you don't want to do. This is your gut communicating with you. The primal visceral feelings we get from our gut are significant. Don't dismiss your intuitive gut feelings. They are accurate and serve as a guidance system as well.

HEART&BRAIN

We have briefly described the brain-mind and the gut-mind; now may I introduce our precious heart-mind. The heart is your feeling centre and it will never deceive you. Our "seeing" perception input from the third eye doesn't always see the truth of what lies before us and can trick us. Things aren't always as we perceive them. All mystics will agree, you can't always trust that which you "see" as truth; but your heart – your feeling centre – will never mislead you. This you can trust. So, I invite you to practice listening to your heart, known as the seat of your soul. If you listen to the noise outside of you (the social media, the news, Hollywood or the opinions of others) you will be pulled off course and begin to question your own soul talk. But if you tune into your heart, you will feel the joy. If you go into your head and try to figure life out, your ego and all your programming will chime in. You will often then feel fear, anxiety, or begin to question yourself.

How will you know the guidance is from your soul, your heart, or your higher team of light, angels, and guides? You will feel excited, expanded, and comfortable with the information and insights you receive. It will just feel right. It might not make perfect logical sense, but it will feel good. For instance, you might get a feeling, see something, or hear something that grabs your attention; or perhaps something makes you feel good or inspires you in some way, or some knowing drops in with 100% certainty. That is a whisper worth waiting for, and your confirmation. I always go to my heart for guidance. That way, I know and trust what I am connecting to. If I feel expansive and good, rather than anxious and contracted, then I know it's all good and aligned. I recommend you do the same. Your heart is your compass; it will never let you down.

There are some nuances to navigate when it comes to listening to your guidance. This does takes practice and focused intention. The human mind is tenacious and we have been trained to use and trust it over our hearts. And our vain imaginations/programs can be so strong that we get 'tricked' into believing it's our inner guidance. I feel it's important to first delineate the difference between being in judgment or discernment. It's a distinction that helped me, and I trust it will help you too. When we are judging, we are using our minds to navigate and calculate what's going on. We make decisions based on preconceived notions and patterns of behaviour, and often our ego jumps in to join the party, too. However, discernment is the practice of using your *body* as your radar, not your mind. This allows you to **tune into the feeling** of what's happening beyond the words, what you see, or the surface situation. You are then perceiving the energy with your whole body – your intelligent heart-mind and gut-mind, not just your brain-mind. Remember, our brain-minds are, for the most part, limited to our programming. However, using your body for discernment is a reliable tool that will never lie. This takes surrender and practice. I know, because it's still in process for me. So be patient; it's not a race.

As you navigate life, people, places, and things, you will begin to take notice of and use this gift of intuition and inner guidance. Your soul will draw you to the right doorway, in a way that is recognizable and resonant to you alone. Trust it, and your body will become a finely tuned instrument of discernment. So, I encourage you to hone your connection to your Soul Self. Guaranteed, it will be the best relationship you cultivate in life. Take time each day for a sacred pause and a Sip of the Divine; in fact, take a big long drink. I invite you to begin the practice of Heart Coherence as taught by the Heart Math Institute, and also found on my YouTube channel (described in detail at the end of the Appendix section of this book). As you begin to feel into your heart and see things through the lens of your soul, using tools such as meditation and affirmative prayer, you'll begin to mature spiritually and life will take on new meaning. You will realize and understand that you've been gifted a sacred body for this life, and your soul is Divine.

Begin to cultivate heart awareness, whether through heart coherence practice, prayer, meditation, or any other method you feel called to; they are critically important, especially in these busy, chaotic times. Your heart is your compass; it's your feeling centre of soul truth. So, I encourage you to be curious, be open, and connect to your heart every day. Don't betray your Higher Soul's knowing. Your heart always knows the next best move for you. Listen, my friend.

I would be amiss if I didn't at least mention that there are other ways to tap into consciousness, guidance, and truth, and ways to navigate interfering fields and leading energies, but they go far beyond the purpose of this book. Years of mentoring and training have made me very adept at Divine muscle testing (also known as applied kinesiology), pendulum use and copper rod dowsing. They are terrific tools as well and worth learning for divining guidance and detecting energy flow. Used properly they can be a great benefit. Maybe my next book will be about teaching these methods?

Why Didn't I Remember All of This Coming Into This Lifetime?

There are many reasons for this general deep forgetting we have about our true spiritual nature when we come into this human life. I'm sure you would agree that life would be a lot easier if we didn't have amnesia about who we really are, and had a road map tucked into our pockets upon arrival. However, that is not the case. I believe this deep forgetting is protective for us. Coming in with full remembrance would probably impinge upon our ability to be fully present and committed to this human life. Our souls came in to have experiences which provide evolution in ways that are only possible in our human bodies on the planet Earth. If we spent our days preoccupied with the beauty of the after-life and being home with the oneness of God, we would have no interest in our body, and the low density, mundane and even difficult experiences of our human existence. Life here on earth can be hard. It is our current job to occupy and fully embody ourselves in this human life experience on this beautiful planet, with fullness and presence. This would not be possible if we were constantly aware of another realm of spiritual existence. The veil between us and the full understanding of our spiritual and multi-dimensional reality is by Divine design.

There is no arguing that life on earth is difficult in ways that life as pure energy and light is not. Here are some Holy writings that explain why forgetting is actually protective. Many would otherwise want to instantly pass over into the heavenly realms if they were fully aware. Adib Taherzadeh, a scholar of the Baha'i faith, recounts a recorded entry from his diary from Baha'u'llah. He says, "God has not endowed the human being, while on this earth, with the ability to perceive even to an infinitesimal measure the conditions of the spiritual worlds of God. If He had, the stability as well as the purpose of this life would have been completely undermined." Baha'u'llah states in one of his tablets that "should the station destined for a true believer in the world beyond be revealed to the extent of a needle's eye, every soul would expire in ecstasy." These writings are a powerful testament to the unimaginable beauty of the spiritual worlds of God, and you can understand why man has been protected with forgetfulness so we can have and complete our soul's mission. I was gifted with such a small glimpse of the other side and I can understand the longing to go home. I find myself frequently longing for the pure state of bliss, love, and expansion in the unified field of God that I experienced, and know is waiting for all of us. I am also abundantly aware of the precious human life I chose to experience for my soul's higher development. Every day I endeavour to be fully embodied and present in this world for as long as is required. It's not always easy.

Soon enough, we'll all be back with Source. Don't preoccupy yourself with getting home. It will happen in Divine timing. We are to focus on our journey here in this sacred human body for the purpose of full presence and soul evolution. We are merging this gap now between awakening to our consciousness and living an elevated experience of Heaven on Earth. The veils are thinning. When life is becoming a big slog, may I remind you that Heaven on Earth is a state of mind – an elevated state of consciousness. As we integrate higher energies, evolving and expanding our awareness, and embodying unconditional love, we are bringing Heaven down to Earth. For now, let's fully embrace the present gifts on this journey, unreservedly offering our energy to the experience we are having right now.

Remembrances to Nourish Your Soul

Before I close out this book, I would like to leave you with a condensed and powerful list of remembrances and some resources in the appendix to assist your journey:

1. Remember that you are a powerful co-creator of your reality.
2. Remember that your words, your thoughts, your emotions shape your reality.
3. Remember that your words and thoughts are energetic codes and frequencies; choose them wisely.
4. Remember that everything is one, we are all connected, nothing is separate.
5. Remember to spend time daily connecting to your Higher Soul Self, cultivate your connection.
6. Remember that each day you start with a clean slate; yesterday is over.
7. Remember that you can change your reality and your vibration within an instant.
8. Remember that you are the soul in charge and you get to choose how you feel.
9. Remember to stay close to God/Source/Creation. It is you, it moves through you, and it's all around you all the time.
10. Remember that you are not and never will be alone.
11. Remember that the body is mortal, your soul is eternal.

12. Remember that you are not here by accident; your soul chose to come here.
13. You are loved, inspired, and supported by your team of light, team of angels, and helpful compassionate spirits.
14. Remember that worry is an exaggerated extension of fear and fear is an illusion.
15. Remember that worrying does not change anything; it weakens the condition of the person doing the worrying and attracts more worry to the thing you are worrying about. Send light and love instead.
16. Remember that in every suffering, one can find meaning and wisdom.
17. Life is full of gifts in "strange wrapping paper."
18. Remember that you are a spirit of pure light and love; you are not your physical body.
19. Remember that the universe will always match your vibration and bring it back 10-fold.
20. Remember that life is Divinely unfolding for you with exact precision, not to you.
21. Remember that you can't get it wrong; it's all just an experience.
22. Remember to always treat yourself with love and compassion.
23. Remember that you are pure light, pure love, formless and connected to all.
24. Remember that death is never an accident, it is always a soul's chosen completion.
25. Remember: YOU ARE THE DIVINE.

I do not proclaim to have all the answers to life, but the above Remembrances are what spirit wants me to bring to you. Outwardly, the world appears precarious, uncertain, and challenging in this present cycle of humanity we are in. It is my hope that this book assists you in having a higher perspective of who you are, and how to navigate your life journey. We are all in this together, evolving through these collective changes and awakenings. Distortions and obstacles that have limited our capacity to perceive and access expanded states of consciousness are falling away.

The clear wave of consciousness is upon us. We are tapping into the collective, united consciousness of all, expanding through the source field of intelligence and accessing our multi-dimensional quantum reality. That was a packed statement; perhaps information for another book! This is an amazing time to be alive.

Each of us are key players in this great adventure. The more we each take responsibility for our own spiritual awareness, healing and growth, the easier it will be for everyone as we move forward into a new chapter for humanity. Let's be real for a moment: everything in our human lives is changing. We are experiencing the transition from Chaos to Sovereignty, and we are being shaken up, woken up, or some might say upgraded. Some of these influences and changes require us to surrender, let go,kk and connect to our truth through stillness, not through striving for more acquisitions and success. Our new reality, if you are open to receiving its truth, is understanding that Heaven isn't a place; it's a state of mind and heart, and a dimension accessible to anyone, anytime. Many like myself have experienced an NDE that lets us know beyond the shadow of a doubt that this is attainable and TRUE. But you don't need an NDE to tap into this truth. Our perceptions of Life and Death are being revolutionized and rebirthed as we awaken. Together we are ushering in the Golden Age of humanity.

Death is not a failure. It's a natural cycle of our souls' evolution. Illness is not a failure. It's the experience our soul has chosen – a conversation and a catalyst for change. Illness is our body's expression of what we hold in our minds, and in our energy field, putting a flashlight on where we are out of balance or have stuck energy. Illness holds it all up to be seen and healed. Our bodies are miracles, and they are working for us to the best of their ability. It's our job to take notice and, with love and compassion, take care and heal.

When your time comes and your story is complete, you will leave your physical body, dropping this illusion of density through which you have expressed yourself in this human journey. You will be rebirthed into the spiritual worlds of God, expressing yourself throughout eternity as a Divine Spirit of truth – endlessly connected to everything, everywhere. You will return home to where only love exists – no fear, no worry, no separation, just pure Divine love, and unified wellness. **That's why I'm not afraid to die.**

We are all here to experience our own story. Love yourself, and be true to yourself. While we're here in human form, we don't have to get lost in the game. We don't have to think, "I'm my job, my circumstances, my infirmity, my lack of income, or my anything." Your first and primary job is to simply remember the truth of who you are. Each and every day, look in the mirror and remember: you are that glowing ball of pure energy.

Enjoy the journey, and may your steps be taken in beauty my friends.

Appendix

> "This day, set the intention to silently converse with the spirit of your heart."
>
> Rev. Michael Beckworth

I offer you some practices that assist me to stay aligned and connected to my Higher Self, stay connected to my heart, and tap into the helpful guidance available across the veil. I hope they serve you well. Please remember, my friends, to filter everything through your own frequency and discernment. Play and have fun.

If you're new to meditation, welcome. We meditate to build resilience, connect with our Higher Selves or other spiritual helpers, to heal, to become more self-aware, to become centered, grounded, relaxed or expansive, and to travel to dimensions. Whatever your reason, I'm sure it all serves to assist us in mastering our lives. When we meditate, we get to choose how we feel. It's like our own biofeedback machine, and an amazing one at that. Relax: meditation is easy; you can't get it wrong. If you show up and participate, you are doing it. Anyone can do it. Even if it's a simple breathing technique. Remember, your life experiences truly come from within, not from your external circumstances. You can cultivate the chemistry of joy, peace, health or whatever you wish, by doing a practice that grows your internal awareness. You are your own pharmacy!

I have a selection of free meditations, heart coherence practices, and tapping sessions on YouTube at Dr. Dawn Cormier; listen and enjoy. There are a gazillion meditations on the internet and YouTube. Begin to explore them and have fun.

3:3:6 Breath

Breath has been the anchor to many spiritual and relaxation practices since the beginning of time. A breathing technique is meditative and can serve to bring you into a deep state of relaxation where your vagus nerve relaxes and recalibrates, bringing you instantly from a state of stress to a parasympathetic state of rest and repair.

Your breath is always with you and available. Let's use it to bring you into the present moment, out of the anxious future and away from your past. Right here, right now.

It's really easy and profound.

Begin by getting yourself in a relaxed position, sitting or lying down. Put your hand on your belly, close your eyes, and relax. Drop your shoulders.

Bring your awareness from the world around you to the world within you. Rest in the awareness of your breath.

~**Breathe in for a count of 3**
 Slowly, deeply into your belly, feel your diaphragm gently press down.
~**Hold or suspend the breath for a count of 3**
 Without tension, disengage your jaw.
~**Exhale for a count of 6**
 Slowly drop all your tension.

Do this a few times, or for 5 minutes, and you will be instantly transported into a relaxed and meditative state.

Practice it. It will work wonders, and it's a great reset for your vagus nerve! It's also a great way to alleviate stress, decompress, or enter into meditation.

Morning Greeting to Great Spirit

O Great Spirit,
I come before you in a humble manner and offer this sacred pipe.
With tears in my eyes and an ancient song of love in my heart I pray:

To the four powers of Creation,
To Grandfather Sun,
To Grandmother Moon,
To Mother Earth,
To my Ancestors.
I pray to the elementals and my relations in nature,
For all those who walk, crawl, fly and swim.
To the seen and unseen, to the good spirits dancing in the light,
I ask that you bless our elders, children, family, friends, and our brothers and sisters who are in need of love and compassion.
I pray for peace amongst the four races of humankind.
I pray for global peace, love, and healing.
May there be beauty above me, beside me, below me, and all around me.
May there be beauty in me.
May the steps I take be those of beauty.
I ask that this world be filled with Peace, Love and Beauty.
And so it is.
Ho.

Adapted from my Aboriginal Therapeutic Touch teacher

Morning Declaration

The intentions and energy you call forth to start your day affect your experience. Intention experiments performed world-wide by famous researchers like Lynn McTaggart, Joe Dispenza, and Bruce Lipton, for example, have shown this to be true on all levels of our lives. No matter what happens in your outside world as our day unfolds, if you greet your day with sacred gratitude, align with your highest good, claim your sovereignty, connect to God Source, and to your heart space, you will do so with awareness and grace because you will know all is working for your highest good. A key fact to remember is, we are at the mercy of our beliefs, not the events or situations that play out in our lives!!

I call forth the Great Source of Consciousness of All That Is.
Archangel Michael, Higher Self, team of angels, team of light and spirit guides, please come to me now; thank you for your continued love, support, and protection.
Divine Mother, I call your in power and presence. Surround me with your Love, Mercy, and Compassion.
I ask to be engaged fully as a light bearer.
May I shine a Divine light so bright that it may illumine the hearts of every person I am in contact with today.
I call forth the Divine protection and healing for all, and Divine guidance and encouragement for all, as to make the world a better place.
Today I claim a day in Heaven.
Today I claim my birthright of health, wealth, and happiness.
Whatever is in the way of this being my reality, I banish it; I uncreate it for my highest and best ways.
I AM the Light that I AM,
And so it is.

Prayer for Spiritual Connection & Support

God is, you are, I AM a spirit of pure love & light.
There is an infinite and all providing love; it's Divine and it's real.
I recognize the existence of Universal Spirit-God.
I AM one with this love and I accept this Presence to be an active and dynamic force in my precious life.
I accept that Universal Love and Divine Love lacks nothing.
I accept my Divine assignment in this lifetime and claim my I AM presence.
I live in alignment with the higher vibrational truth of who I AM.
I acknowledge that I am the object of God's positive attention and unconditional love.
I am appreciating God's continual gaze and guidance on behalf of my wellbeing.
Today, no matter where I am, no matter where I am going, no matter what I am doing, I will be in conscious awareness that God is here with me!!!

God is guiding me, appreciating me, supporting me, loving me, assisting me, inspiring me, acknowledging me, having fun with me, helping me, uplifting me.
I affirm and trust the consciousness of all and I call for the highest consciousness that I AM.

Declaration of your I AM Presence

I know who I AM in Truth
I know what I AM in Truth
I know how I serve in Truth
God Is, I AM Free

From Paul Selig

Gratitude for Divine Presence

Thank you for surrounding me in your love and light
Thank you for protecting me in your love and light
Thank you for imbuing me with your love and light

From Michael Sandler

Calling in the Angels

The angels are all around you, all the time, just waiting to be active in your life. Various angelic supports come and go, but your guardian angel never leaves your side even for a second! Angels are here to assist you, but you must ask them and invite them in. Ask for help from the spiritual planes; they can help shift your energy so you live and come from a place of higher elevation. Ask for assistance, guidance, or an energetic boost. It can be as simple as this invitation:
<u>Simply say:</u> *"I would like to get into vibrational alignment with the angels,"* then ask for whatever it is you desire, ending with "Thank you."

Awakened Consciousness Prayer

Take a deep centering breath, connect to your heart space, connect to Mother Gaia (below), connect to the heavens (above), now bring both sacred presences in meeting at your heart space; as above and so below.

<u>Say out loud or in your heart:</u>
I call forth the assistance of all higher beings in the realms of service to the Christed crystalline energy & consciousness to assist us at this time. May I/we be surrounded and supported with the legions of light angels to release and dissolve any and all pain, trauma, wounds, misinformation and distortions in all time and space with Divine guidance, ease, speed, and grace.

To the Archangels of light, if there is any discourse or heavy energies in my presence or energy field that is not for my highest good, let the light of Divine love dispel them now as I prepare towards 5th dimensional Unity consciousness.

I call forth healing for all aspects of my mind, body, and spirit that require healing at this time for my highest good. I fully embrace and embody my spirit in this sacred human temple, as I move along the ascension pathway with joy, grace, love, and wisdom.

I call forth my traumas, fears, doubts, shame, or any vibration that is not serving me for my highest good to be held in the light, to be transmuted and neutralized by my team of light. I send light and love to all aspects of myself.

I pray that the forces of Divine love, harmony, and peace be infused into the spaciousness of my cleansed energy field and body, so that it be filled with this power.

I pray for the strength to embody these fields of Divine light, move them through me in the presence of love, peace, and healing, and into the earth as she continues her journey of ascension. As I am joined by angelic forces of God's light, I express my gratitude and support, for as one is lifted up, we are all lifted up.

I declare that my human pattern is now open to this exalted Divine energy and light, to consummate Unity consciousness in my being, fully

embodied in this precious temple of my body, knowing that as I cross the threshold to fully awakened 5th dimensional consciousness, I am supported in your loving embrace of Divine love and light.
May I bring more peace and joy to the world and benefit the planet.
Easily and gently, with love and wisdom,
and so it is.
Done in Beauty.

Transforming Worry into Peace and Acceptance

Every human emotion holds a frequency; everything in our universe is a frequency. Everyone feels worry at some point and as mentioned earlier in the book, worry doesn't serve to improve any outcome. When we choose to worry, we weaken our bodies and attract more stress and the low vibration of worry to ourselves and to the person or event we are worrying about. The good news is there are ways to transform worry so that instead of having a deleterious effect, we can have a positive and healing effect.

Method one: Awareness

The first step is to become aware, without judgment, that you are worrying. Say to yourself, "Whoops, there I go again." Now, let's make a lateral shift. Using the power of your imagination, instead of imagining the worst possible outcome, visualize your loved one or the event bathed in white or golden light. See it clearly in your mind's eye. Imagine the angels or guides watching over the person or situation. Generate a feeling of love and peace, and now send that light to them or the situation instead of sending the vibration of worry. There you go – you've just infused them with higher vibrational light which will serve them or the situation in a helpful positive way. Whenever you are feeling helpless, frightened, or worried, you can always help by sending love and light. The energy of worry or fear is never beneficial to anyone.

Method two: Heart Command

This method is based on Elizabeth Wood's insight and work on *the three brains* (mind, heart, and gut). She has graciously made this available to the whole world and wants it to be shared. This is my absolute favourite method to transform an emotion easily, quickly, and effectively in the moment. It's called a heart command and she has given permission to share it with the world.

Heart Command - put your hand on your heart, become centered, and say the following:

"Dear heart, please *lift* from my body and field the frequency of <u>Worry (or pick your own)</u>, NOW." Take a deep breath.

"Dear heart, please *fill* my body and field with the frequency of <u>Peace (or pick your own)</u>, NOW." Take a deep breath.

You can do this method for any emotion or frequency you wish to transmute. You are Source energy and you can shift energy easily. Try it out and you will be surprised how effective it is. You can change your state within 30 seconds. I suggest not doing more than 4 heart commands a day, as shifting too much energy can be overwhelming.

Sip of the Divine

This is a practice of putting your attention and intention on connecting to your Divine self. This is the magic. Suzanne Giesemann coined the term Sip of the Divine, and I think it's brilliant. There are many ways to connect daily with our Soul and Divine nature. Whichever way you choose to commune is completely up to you. Just do it!

Sit or lie down comfortably. Put your hand on your heart. Take some long relaxing breaths to get centered. Go within, draw your attention away from where you came, where you're going after this, and just be here in your body, now in the present moment. Slow your exhalations to shift your body out of sympathetic state to a relaxed healing state.

Focus your attention on your heart, the seat of your soul. Reverently and lovingly, with your hand over your heart, ask to be in connection with your higher realm. You are never alone; you always have help. You always have contact with the other side of the veil. Becoming aware of this reality will tune you in.

Now tune into the guidance that's available to you. Ask that the guides here for your highest good step forward and then trust in their support. Now ask for a sign to recognize when they are trying to communicate or get your attention. Ask for something particular like a specific colour, a word, a symbol, a sound, some lyrics… something that you will recognize. Let it come easily, don't force it. When something pops into your awareness, give thanks.

Now go on with your day. Be aware when that sign is shown to you. Pay attention. This is how your guides talk to you, support you, love you, and communicate with you. Start to cultivate a connection, ask questions, stay in your heart, don't go into your mind, don't let your ego chase answers. Be in your heart. Your heart always knows your best next steps. Always be grateful.

Blessing Everything Meditation

This is a powerful practice; I promise your life and health will change by doing this.

Read the instructions then run the practice yourself. Don't worry if you miss a step or don't get the words or phrases right; it's the feeling that counts. Listen to nice music, or in silence, get comfortable and enjoy. You can bless everything and anything.

Enter into your Holy space;
Open your sacred heart;
Place your hand on your heart and pause into this holy space;
Put a smile on your face.
Call on Mother Mary, and ask for her assistance;
Thank her for her love, compassion, and mercy.
Ask to connect with your I AM Presence;
Breathe deeply and open your heart:
"To the beloved mother of all life, I am open to receive your blessing today."
Let go of all preconceived ideas, judgments, and ideas;
Open yourself to the power of Holy Presence.
Give thanks.
Call your angels of light to be with you, surround you and support you;

Today bring all of your concerns and put them on the altar, give them over, unburden yourself;
All your aches and pains, any appearance of sickness, put them on the altar;
All concerns about your body, put them on the altar;
Breathe;
Your body is holy and sacred;
Your body is the vehicle of ascension;
Forgive yourself from seeing your body as separate from your Divine source.
Allow the healing ray of emerald green to flood your body on the altar;
Breathe in the green ray of healing, surrounding you now;
The healing green ray is assisted by Archangel Raphael.
Ask Archangel Raphael to bless every aspect of your body;
This is the age of the violet flame, the purifying transmuting flame of St. Germain:
"I give you full command to help me bless everything I see today.
I am grateful for your presence and honour and thank you for your healing.
Bring the violet flame in full measure into my body,
Blessing and lighting up every element in my body, my cells, atoms, electrons,
Blessing the water in my body, the minerals."
Bring the cool violet flame into every aspect of your body.
Use your hands to bless your body; with reverence touch any part of your body that needs assistance; feel the warmth of the energy.
Say "I bless my beloved body – thank you for this vehicle that houses my soul;
Bless my body from the bottom of my feet to the top of my head."
Bless the room you are in, bless everything in it;
Bless your household, bless everyone seen and unseen that are with you every day;
Bless your yard, your neighborhood, your country;
Bless the angels with you now and in the future;
Bless the trees, the grass, the water, the air;
Breathe in the blessed air;
Feel the violet flame; ask it to purify everything you are blessing.

Be thankful for everything, even things that are hurting, things that are hard for you.
Bless everyone in the world;
Bless your body with the violet flame;
Feel the violet light expanding everywhere;
May you be blessed.
Continue to give thanks and give blessings to everything you can imagine and especially yourself.

Healing "I am Word" Declaration

This declaration is claiming your reality as a Divine Being, knowing that the reality you exist in is malleable to your thoughts and intentions. As you claim this, you put into gear the systems required to shift your body and awareness. You are informing your body with new frequency and information to heal.

"I am Word through my frequency;
I am Word through my body;
I see myself in perfect form, I am healthy and healed;
I am now choosing to know that which would support my healing;
I am lifting my vibration;
I am now choosing to know my body as a joyful vehicle and I am celebrating it in Divine love and thanking it for being with me on this remarkable journey in consciousness;
I am choosing to realign my energies in perfect ways for my highest good,
And I am knowing myself as an aspect of the Divine.
I am Word through this intention; Word I am Word."

Extrapolated from Paul Selig's work

Heart Coherence Practice

I have an easy and profound YouTube recording on the practice of Heart Coherence that can help you become skilled at listening to your heart. Below are instructions for your benefit. This technique was developed over a quarter century ago by the Heart Math Institute. It has scientific data supporting the fact that everything starts in the heart field, not the brain. Signals from the heart influence the brain, not the other way around. The Heart Coherence Practice is very simple yet profound; don't underestimate its power. Once you learn and cultivate this practice to regulate your nervous system and bring your heart and brain into a coherent 0.1 Hz frequency, you have mastered your energy. You are no longer a victim of outside influences and events; you get to choose your predominant frequency. You will be calm and centered. It has been shown to reduce over 13,000 biological stress responses in the body. It's my favorite and an absolute necessity in my opinion.

This practice teaches you how to engage your heart in three simple steps:
- a heart awareness
- a heart breathing
- a heart feeling

Instructions:
Close your eyes, drop your shoulders, put a smile on your face and shift your awareness from your thinking mind into your feeling heart; it's time to go inside.

1. Heart focus: focus your attention on your heart area. If you touch your heart with two fingers or place your palm over your heart centre, your attention will automatically go there. Start to become aware of your breath, slow it down, breathe a little deeper than normal into your heart space, in for 4 seconds & out 5-6 seconds. Breathing like this tells your body you are safe.

2. Heart breathing: now imagine breathing through your heart. Breathe life into your heart space. Picture yourself slowly breathing in and out through your heart area, front, back and sides. You can imagine a colour of pink or gold if you desire. Grow the light of your heart.

3. Heart feeling: now activate a positive feeling as you maintain your heart focus and breathing. To the best of your ability focus on ***caring, gratitude, appreciation, or compassion***. It may help you to recall a time you felt good inside, or recall someone you care about or are grateful for; try to re-experience the ***feeling***. Remember a special place, time or event or the love you feel for a beloved, a friend, or a pet. The key is to focus on something you really appreciate. Hold the focus on the feeling! Well done! You've created a coherent energy from your heart to your brain. How do you feel? Notice a greater sense of ease, wellbeing, or relaxation?

I trust that these prayers, invocations, declarations, meditations, and tools will assist you in living your Higher Soul Self as they have helped me. Call in the magic and power that you are, my friends.

May your path to Spiritual Awakening be blessed, and always remember to live in Faith, not Fear.

Many Blessings

Manufactured by Amazon.ca
Bolton, ON